Light Bites

A Lighthearted Look at Everyday Life

Terri Houston

All accounts in this book are based on what I remember or what I concocted. Email comments to LiteBites777@gmail.com

Copyright © 2021 by Terri Houston
All Rights reserved.

Of course, no copyright infringement intended.

for Dick

Acknowledgements

A bazillion thanks to Glenn Houston, who edited with care, humor, and attention that can only be found in a retired nuclear physicist.

Thanks to my dear friends, who made these stories and associated smiles happen.

Many images gratefully acknowledged from Pixabay.

Epilogue

In the spirit of *eat dessert first*, the epilogue is served in the front of this book. Of course, an epilogue is normally in the back of a book and serves to wrap up loose ends. So if you never get to the back of this book, which is a very real possibility, you'll find satisfaction in having any dangling mysteries cleaned up right here and right now.

You're welcome.

Writing a book is a common bucket-list item, and my list is no exception. As a kid, I remember my family beaming with pride when they talked about my great-great uncle, John E. Barrett, who authored a book, "Red Shadow, A Romance of the Wyoming Valley." It was published in 1913, and I remember very clearly the dark green cover adorned with an Indian in full headdress.

As I grew up and became mildly interested in my Irish heritage, I learned the reason that many great writers were Irish is because they didn't have much money, and writing is pretty much free. You don't need special clothing or equipment, and unless you want to professionally print your works, all it takes is a pen and paper—or computer if you don't know how to use a pen.

My writing journey started when I was very young. I cut up sheets of paper and stapled them together to form a booklet. It was written and illustrated for my friend and recounted silly situations that we lived through and laughed about. The title was very non-creative: *My Friend*. Fifty years later, I cut up more paper and sent *My Friend III* to my friend as a gift for her retirement. Fortunately, she's very easy to please, which is the main reason why we've been friends for decades.

My engineering career was interrupted by a 2-year sabbatical as a technical editor for a trade journal. That's a magazine you don't remember asking for and nothing at all would get your name off of the mailing list. During that time, I started to freelance for other technical magazines, but needed a pen name since you don't want the company paying your health benefits finding out that you're moonlighting for the competition. Kelly Barrett was the name I chose in honor of the author in my lineage, and I had great fun writing monthly articles about the latest marvels in the electronics industry.

I thought I was doing a good job, but when I announced to the magazine editor that I was leaving to go back to work as an engineer, I remember Ernie's words very clearly. He said, "Thank God."

I don't know if my sister Ann had 'author' on her bucket list, but she sent my brother paper copies of a boatload of poems she wrote—with a pen—over the years. Glenn published them in a very nice paperback using artwork from Michelangelo and Ann, and sent me a copy. It is wonderful, and I'm not saying that because she's my sister.

That book was the motivation I needed to complete this book. I'll assume if you're reading this, I did actually complete it. Besides crossing one item off my bucket list, my hope for this book is that some of the chapters make you smile.

By the way, if you want to read the Foreword, you'll find it at the end of the book.

Contents

Those Around Us
Are You Asleep?	2
Recyclables Speak Volumes	4
What Did You Say?	6
I'll Have What She's Having	8
Drivers: Pay Attention to those Lights!	10
Glass Kisses	12
In the Right Direction	14
Advisory Committee	16
One's Enough	18
Photos Finished	20

Society's Quirks
Too Many Choices	24
Battle of the Gases	26
Running Behind	28
A Word from our Sponsors	30
Gated Communities	32
The Best Superpower	34
The Lullaby of Broadway	36
Pick Me	38
License and Registration	40
About Face	42

Aging Affects the Young
Waist Not, Why Not?	46
A Fondness for Memories	48
Two Piece or Not Two Piece	50
Coming of Age	52
Mattresses' Sinking Feeling	54
Find a Penny	56
Game Time	58
Raising a Green Thumb	60
Nothing Close to the Truth	62
Wisdom with Age	64

Look at it This Way
My Favorite Holiday	68
Actually, Numbers Do Lie	70
Mourning the Soap Loss	72
It's Time	74
Can't Find the Words	76
My Favorite Hobby	78
On a Roll	80
Shower Power	82
Buon Appetito	84
One Ripe Banana	86

All Work
Stringy Email	90
She Can Act, Too	92
Alternate Reality	94
The Interview	96
Office Health	98
Truth, Straight Up	100
The Loud One	102
Those Entitled	104
Working on Retirement	106
Are You Done Yet?	108

x

Lite Bites

Those Around Us

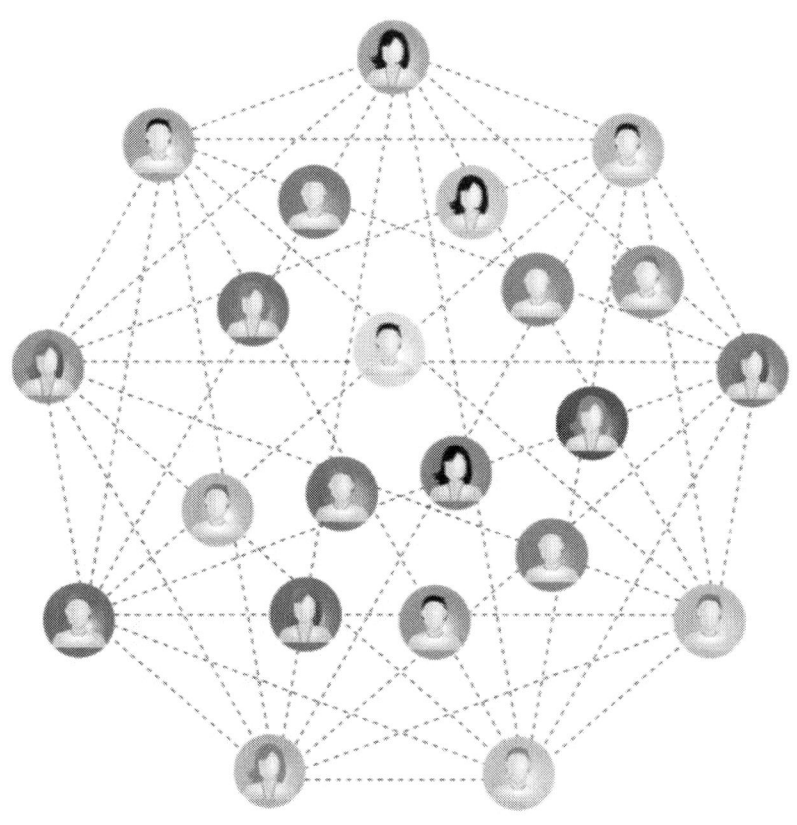

Lite Bites

Are You Asleep?

If someone offers you a million dollars to identify the most absurd question ever asked, you'll win if you reply "Are you asleep?" I know this because I've been asked it many a time, and it has the unique feature of getting dumber each time. Sometimes, I've learned, it's asked two or three times before there is a response.

The situation is always the same—my eyes are closed, I'm not moving and the surroundings are quiet. Sometimes it's 5:30 a.m. and I'm lying peacefully in bed. Other times, it's late at night while I sit in the passenger seat of a moving car and my head is drooped over like a rag doll.

The questioner is the man of my dreams, or rather my interrupted dreams, and the *he-who-only-needs-five-hours-a-night* kind of guy. He's lonely and he wants some company, and he wants that company to be conscience and engaged in coherent if not lively conversation.

My answer to this absurd question has changed over the quarter century of being asked. In the early days, the answer was a startled "What's wrong!?" The middle years' answer has been a disgruntled "Not anymore." Knowing that a lack of a response just means the question gets repeated, my current, age-of-enlightenment answer is "Yes."

However, once the senseless question is asked and the slumber is broken, the *you-can-sleep-all-you-want-when-you're-dead* guy is ready with more questions: Why is your face puffy? Why do you have one eye closed? What do you want to talk about?

Lite Bites

Studies show that money and sex are the two topics that cause couples to argue the most. I say those who did the study closed their eyes to the obvious compatibility metric between people—the number of hours in a day when you are willing to be communicative. It should be evident that number decreases on weekends. Nothing wreaks havoc on Sunday morning slumber more than the 5 a.m. query, "When are you going to get out of bed so we can change the sheets?"

A glorious equalizer happens during summer vacations. *Mr. Rise-n-Shine* awakes at 4 a.m. to go fishing. I sleep in. He returns three or four hours later to someone fully awake, groomed and ready for the day. When the fish stench is washed away, we make breakfast plans and enjoy each other's company throughout the day. By late evening, we're in sleep sync and ready to hit the feathers at the same time.

The subject of napping must be addressed here. Babies nap. Old people nap. Young geniuses who work at Microsoft are allowed to nap since it's been shown that they are more productive afterwards. So how do I convince my naps-are-for-wimps guy that, except for perils to life and limb, the napper should never be questioned while the nap is in progress? I've tried to no avail.

There are some people who have trouble with sleep. Others revel in the relaxation and enjoyment of shut eye. I am the latter type—always have been. And whenever I see my *let's-get-up-real-early-tomorrow* guy taking an infrequent nap on a lazy summer afternoon, I know that deep down inside he wants to be just like me.

Recyclables Speak Volumes

 If you want to know everything important about your neighbors, just take a walk around the block when the recyclables are set out for pick up. Someone clever once said that the eyes are the windows to the soul, but eyes are nothing compared to a bin full of discarded bottles, cans, and cartons that are a microscope on daily life.

Empty food and beverage containers offer better insight into a family's life than their video streaming because bins capture the crucial highlights. You don't need to be bothered with hours of boring daily activities. Those tubs adorned with three bent arrows are the Cliff's Notes, so to speak, of living in the 'burbs. Trash destined for their afterlife can confirm what's already known or provide insight into a hidden household personality.

The *party house* has empty gin bottles—many of them—mixed among wine bottles so big that the handles are built right into the neck. Mini bottles of club soda and tonic water make up the remaining volume. There's nary an empty soup can or juice bottle. It makes you wonder if the producers of the recyclables analyze it themselves. "Honey, the bin goes out once a week and we have five empty Boodles Gin bottles in each load. Should we be inviting more friends over?"

Then there's the *beer guy*'s bin with dozens of lite cans that can't possibly fit into the tub, so they get crushed before loading. The *single lady* produces so little plastic recycling that the paper recycling gets nested on the top, hiding any tidbits of her solitary story. Her eating and drinking habits remain a deep, dark secret, but we know she finishes the newspaper's crossword puzzle—the hard one—every day.

It's not easy these days to know what is salvageable and what is not. Even if you read the arcane recycling rules, it's still hard to judge what containers need to go to a landfill and which ones can get reincarnated to help save the planet. In my household, the fate of the half-gallon OJ cardboard cartons caused heated debate until the recycling company distributed refrigerator magnets with a cartoon of my cardboard carton tossed in the tub with a smiley face nearby. What about those black plastic sushi trays with a number 6 on them? We don't know if our local recycler is technically competent enough to handle all the way up to 6 types of manmade trays, so sometimes they go in, other times they go in the regular trash.

During a recent jaunt around the neighborhood, we wondered how our newly single neighbor was faring. A glance into the recycle bin made us glad. It held lots and lots of Amazon Prime boxes. Nothing soothes a fresh separation like a shopping spree to fill your house with all the stuff *you* like. When said neighbor popped out with even more Amazon boxes that wouldn't fit in the bin, there were bright smiles and small talk about what a beautiful day it was. Our neighbor is going to be just fine.

One of the most dejecting moments in life is when your recyclables get rejected. How does it make sense that almost all cleaning-supply containers can be reincarnated, but their caps are just regular trash? After seeing a half-dozen screw caps remaining in our otherwise emptied bin with a "Dear John" *note* from our recycling company, we've learned our lesson. It could be worse—there's a trash collection company with the motto: "Satisfaction Guaranteed or Double your Garbage Back."

What Did You Say?

I know the man of my dreams so well that I can tell you how he'll respond to anything I say when we start a conversation. I also know how he'll answer any of his friends or family. This is easy because his response will always be the same. Even if I said, "The house is on fire," the response would be, "What?"

He says I'm not talking loud enough. I say he's not listening hard enough. The truth is that his response is done unconsciously; it's in the genetic makeup that was handed down from his mother to create a mental carriage return. It delayed the time to get engaged in conversation so she could be prepared to take in the data. Anna had much more annoying traits, so I'm just glad her son doesn't collect those little papers stapled to the end of every Red Rose tea bag he's ever used. But the *What* thing can be annoying.

"What?" is the response when he's deeply embroiled in the sports section of the newspaper, running through stats from last night's ball games, and asked whether he wants more coffee. It's also the answer when he's waiting for the Weather Channel to deliver critical information to determine if the orchids need to be pulled inside for the night while I'm asking something about the edible status of the beans in the refrigerator.

"What?" is also the verbal red flag that appears when you think you're engaged in a two-way conversation, but he's thinking about a late-night snack, although his eyes are staring into yours and you were communicating just a few moments ago.

Fortunately, management of the timing of *What* can be easily handled by inserting your own mental 'start your engines' signal. Just begin each conversation with "Hey."

It goes like this:
"Hey."
"What?"
"Did you get the phone bill yet because I think it's due just about now."
"Let me check."

You'll note in this example that an explanation of the question being asked must be included in the question to forgo the aggravating follow-up *'Why?'* It's good practice when you have the floor to get in all the pertinent data in the fewest words possible before the onset of mind drift to something more interesting. It's an effective method to get to the point rather quickly and eliminate repetition. Without this technique, the conversation would be:
"Did you get the phone bill yet?"
"What?"
"I said did you get the phone bill yet?"
"Why?"
"Because I think it's due."
"When?"
"It was due about this time last month."
"What?"
"The phone bill. It should be due about now, can you see if we got it yet?"
"Let me check."

See the difference? The key to better communication was taught to me in the first 10 seconds of a news writing class: prepare, grab your readers' attention, and quickly get your message in before they turn to the comics.

Lite Bites

I'll Have What She's Having

One of the best ways to determine if you'll become fast friends with a new couple is to go to dinner with them. It's the best couple-date scenario because it brings into play many different aspects of their joint personality that will determine compatibility. Will they arrive on time? Order cocktails? Choose the most or least expensive items on the menu? Can they understand the menu? Are they stingy or generous tippers? Can she hold a conversation while twirling spaghetti? Will he keep his mouth closed while chewing? You'll know whether you want to spend more time with these folks well before the dessert decision is made. Trust me on this one.

A couple who believes that fine dining includes toting your tray of food while searching for an empty table will just not be compatible with one who considers themselves 'foodies' and will travel great distances, perform thorough research and make reservations weeks in advance to enjoy a meal. It's been proven by some scientific study that people who take great pleasure in eating have more taste buds than those who can't tell if they're dining at Denny's or Tavern on the Green.[1]

The taste-bud-count information came to light for us during the "toying with getting into the wine business" phase. After meeting people who can sip a wine and precisely identify the varietal, region, and year of the grape harvest, you realize there are folks with sensory ability beyond the imaginable. Let's leave these savants for a minute and discuss more regular folks.

---

[1] A swanky eatery in New York City's Central Park

One couple we know will happily join us at any restaurant we suggest, but they always order chicken. He likes chicken with hot-as-hell sauce on it. She eats chicken with a salad. Another couple has an interesting quirk. She'll order, and then he says, "That sounds good, I'll have the same thing she's having." He doesn't even open the menu. He reasons that he's never been disappointed with what she orders, and when they eat at home, they both have the same thing, anyway. I think I'm on to him, though. He does this so she won't be eating off his plate.

One of the reasons to eat out with others is to taste what they ordered and judge who made the best choice. I just can't resist stabbing my fork into an attractive morsel that may happen to be on someone else's plate. Don't worry; I make sure the fork is clean. For those that need to be introduced to my habit, I'll first ask lots of questions about how they're enjoying their veal or salmon or potato puff. Before things get awkward, I offer a taste of my meal, at which point they usually give in and offer a bite of theirs. A few couple dates later, they learn to accept and reciprocate in kind without going through the questions and awkward phase routine.

The latest study says people eat out 4.2 meals every week. If you're feeling out a new couple and are too leery to suggest a full dinner, try the 0.2 meal and just go for ice cream.

Lite Bites

Drivers: Pay Attention to Those Lights!

We've all seen drivers who are listening to loud music, seat dancing and only touching the steering wheel for a quick course correction. One such driver I spotted recently was moving much below the speed limit—too engrossed in getting their groove on to notice all traffic passing by. When I passed by, I couldn't help but notice the yellow light glowing brightly on the dashboard. I'm sure it was the light that warns you that it's time to check your engine. I was amazed that someone could treat such a blaring warning with such nonchalance and drive along in an apparent good mood when their car is begging for attention in the only way a car can beg.

The reason I'm amazed is because I stared at such a red-orange light for months, and it drove me to distraction. The car manual says there are numerous reasons why this light comes on—from a gas cap that wasn't replaced properly to an intermittent problem that will go away in time. Blogs on this subject (there are blogs on this subject) reveal there are 247 conditions that can make that light come on. Information on how to make it turn off is available, but not too helpful. Maybe your gas cap is loose. Maybe you had bad gas. Maybe you're low on oil. Or just maybe your catalytic converter has gone bad, which is as costly as it sounds.

A fair part of our population is driving around with the Check Engine light lit and the reason is simple—mechanics can't figure out what causes it to come on, and the car doesn't seem to show any loss of function even though this warning shines in your eyes. In three previous trips to the shop my mechanic replaced just about everything that would cause any of the 240 reasons for this light to glow. The fourth trip was the tipping point, so he offered a rental so he could spend even more time troubleshooting. This warning light was not going to get the best of him. The only rental I could get was a Ford F-150 truck that surely was used for transporting livestock based on the aroma and the stains on the seats, but it was complimentary, so I muffled my complaints.

The shop called three days later to announce my Check Engine light was off and my engine was running smoothly, just as it was, by the way, with the light shining. When I got my ride back, the red-orange light was indeed off, and I was assured the cause was found and addressed. I asked for the results of the investigation from the office worker who was busy stapling lots of paper that showed a $0 balance due. She mumbled something about how great it was that the problem was finally corrected, so I didn't press for more information.

I'll never know what caused that light to shine. My car ran fine, but the manual said it was something that shouldn't be ignored. Something was indeed awry, and it would be nice to know which of the 247 conditions my car suffered from. I'm betting it was the condition where the light went bad and was just stuck in the 'on' mode.

Lite Bites

Glass Kisses

 Art is not only in the eye of the beholder, it also hangs from a chain around my neck. And it was what Lindsey pointed to when she screamed, "My dad made that!" But that's the middle of the story, so let me start from the beginning.

Friends Barbara and Ed were visiting for a few days. Since they're our artsy friends, a trip to Chihuly's glass museum was in order. If you don't know Chihuly, he's a famous glass maker who lost sight in one eye due to a car accident. His pieces are recognized throughout the world, most notably filling the ceiling of the Bellagio Casino in Las Vegas. I find them beautiful in the way they capture light and color. Barbara and I were performing the requisite stroll through the gift shop after seeing jaw-dropping glass creations in the museum when we spotted the only thing we could afford: colorful glass pieces shaped like Hershey Kisses. We didn't know what we'd do with them, but we each bought a few as mementos of our visit.

I found a sturdy chain and wore a kiss as a pendent to work. It was heavy, but unique and colorful and I received many compliments. A co-worker, Lindsey, noticed my kiss and said her dad made it. Lindsey is a lovable eccentric, so I didn't think much of it until she explained her dad has a local "hot shop" and makes those kisses by the bucketful and they're sold in gift shops all around. Turns out, this was all true. Her dad, Chuck Boux, made the kisses! Mr. Boux's name is not as recognizable as Chihuly, but I'd say his talent is comparable. Lindsey was kind enough to give me a bunch of kisses in all different colors. I thought it would be nice to share my good luck with other gals who may also like them, so I mailed them around the US with a note about the legend of the glass kiss.

The legend goes that if you get a glass kiss from someone who cares about you and it makes you smile, it will give you magical power. Just bring the kiss to a sunny place and hold it in your hand while you close your eyes and make a wish about someone you care about. That wish will eventually come true. Maybe not immediately, but some day your wish will come true for that other person. Kinda like Dorothy's red slippers, but not so selfish and without the annoying heel clicking.

Of course, this legend is a bunch of hooey since I made it all up, but it made for a good note to mail along with the kisses. Except when I sent it to Barbara, who became sullen. She thought the kisses were made by Dale Chihuly himself. That's what she told everyone when showing off her glass artwork. Deep down, she kind of knew that maybe that wasn't true, but she was hoping they were created by one of his staff while under the watchful remaining eye of the master himself.

To console her, it was time for me to explain my dogma of intentions. When you're not telling the truth, and you know it's not the truth, then you get a black mark. When you're not telling the truth, but honestly believe it could very well be true, it's in the *no harm/no foul* category, and you can continue to tell that untruth so long as your story doesn't change and no one gets hurt. And if she held a kiss with her eyes closed in a sunny place and wished for something good to happen to the receiver of the untruth, she'd get 10 bonus points when the wish actually came true.

In the Right Direction

I'm not ashamed to admit that I'm directionally challenged, so I frequently use my GPS even on trips I've made a number of times, even the commute to the office. This was a daily trip I used to make before working from home became fashionable and necessary, and my GPS would be fired up on both the *to* and *from* legs five days a week. On many occasions, I was given advanced notice of a traffic delay and guided along back streets to arrive at my destination earlier than if I was on auto pilot.

Sometimes I'd be in highway daze and my GPS would shout that my exit was coming up. Other times, the GPS would become confused and lead me down a dead end or circling in loops before I realized it didn't know where to go either. I'll admit that the GPS map installed when I bought the car is woefully out of date, so there are times when I'm driving on pavement but my GPS didn't get the message that the path is a legitimate route, so it shows my car icon moving on blankness.

On the flip side, my sweetie is known for having a GPS in his head. I often hear the story of his parents asking *him* for directions, even when he was very young, on trips they made just once before. His recall of lefts and rights was right on. He just shrugs at this skill and claims to have a *travelgraphic* memory.

So, you can imagine what happens when I load an address into the GPS when I'm driving my better half to a place we've been a few times before. "What are you doing? You know how to get there," he says. "Actually, I don't," I respond, but he can't believe me. The GPS wants me to turn left. "You need to make a right here," says the guy riding shotgun. Obediently I turn right, the GPS recalculates the route, then says our ETA is a few minutes less than if I dutifully followed its previous course. Then comes the I-told-you-so look. It's comforting to know that if I don't follow the GPS, it retreats into recalculating mode, and will repeat this loop the same number of times that you ignore its directions—without any bad looks.

When you're going somewhere you've never been before, my best advice is to check the weather at the same time you find the address. Inclement weather is tied directly to squirrely directions because the GPS can't get the guidance from the satellites that are blocked by a layer of rain and clouds. My first encounter with this was years ago when my GPS actually said, "Poor signal, travel to a location with better reception." It could not tell me where to go unless I went somewhere else first. That's when I gave it a very bad look, along with some verbal direction on where it could stick its algorithms.

The whole directional debate escalates to another level when traveling with others. When I'm behind the wheel, I turn to the GPS, but everyone else feels they know the way to San Jose, so to say. The reason I follow the GPS is that after a few well-meaning go-lefts and stay-straights, the passengers get sidetracked in conversation and ignore their navigation duties. Rather than hearing, "Oh no, you should have exited 8 miles back," I just trust in my electronic director and eventually get to our intended locale. And that's a move in the right direction.

Advisory Committee

The saying "None of us is as smart as all of us," is attributed to Kenneth H. Blanchard and some proverb-writing Japanese guy, but no truer words were spoken. If you are lucky to have an advisory council at your **disposal, you're likely sailing through life without speedbumps** (and without worrying about mixed metaphors.) **If you don't have such a group on hand, don't fret**—just come to my community's water-aerobics classes.

Nothing is smarter than a group of semi- and fully retired semi-dressed ladies who have seen it all, collectively speaking. During my second class, I complained of night leg cramps. My aquatic ad-hoc medical team advised magnesium, including dosage, what time of day to take it, and how much fluid to drink with the dose. Cramps were gone in two days. How about the common leaky roof? Where should visiting grandkids sleep? Who are the good mechanics? Tax advice? Best-fitting bathing suits? When is it time for hip replacement? The recommendations flow freely and emphatically and typically with multiple confirmations. You receive sound and tested advice in a resort-like setting while you work off some calories. How great is that?

These welcoming broads have a broad span of life experiences. Some were in the medical field. Some were teachers. Just like **most Floridians, many are from 'up north.' The kind Irish lady talks** a lot during class, which suits me just fine since I can listen to her lilting brogue all day long. Some ladies just come to talk to each other during class—perfectly OK. Some sing along to the Disney tunes that play when our DJ happens to pick that genre. This class is the perfect meld of socializing, exercising, cooling off, and enjoying pleasant sunny mornings. I am very grateful to the two ladies who lead the class and arrange music at the perfectly appropriate beats-per-minute tempo.

While this pool of women has a free flow of sage advice, there is a flip side to this dynamic. I propose that "None of us is as dumb as all of us" describes how a group of people asked to make a decision will compromise their beliefs to arrive at a consensus that anyone with half a brain would see is ridiculous. Sometimes called Groupthink, individuals stuck in a room and asked to solve a problem don't want to stray from the herd or cause controversy, so the solution such a group offers turns out to be group junk.

There's been more than one study, supported by that famous game show, to suggest the fastest path to an optimum solution is finding a competent *individual* and allow them to phone a few friends or ask the audience for advice. However, if you turn this around and have a group work as a team to solve a problem, the team will try to placate everyone and their solution will be pure bunk. Take note business world: empowering an individual to come up with a process, solution, or location for the company holiday party, is a cheaper and quicker path to a right decision when there are quite a few acceptable solutions and just as many paths to failure.

There may be no "I" in team, but there's no common sense, either. I'll see you at the pool.

Lite Bites

One's Enough

Anyone who eats has visited a grocery store. Everyone who has visited a grocery store has fallen into the trap of the irresistible buy-one-get-one, or BOGO to its friends. And we all know deep down that we're paying more for the one item you need just to get a second one that you don't. But that won't stop us from tossing twins into our grocery cart and wheeling away feeling like we got a good deal.

Sometimes it makes sense. Bagels don't last long in my house, and freezing the second package for the near future is a good strategy. Big mustards do not make sense. There are only three recipes that use mustard, and how many hot dogs can you eat anyhow? Even though it has a long shelf life, buying two 32-oz bottles of mustard makes you want to toss out the first bottle, even though it's almost full, because it's been in the refrigerator way too long and the nozzle becomes icky. Besides, there's another one in the cupboard to replace it. This whole scenario just doesn't cut the mustard.

Another grocery overload happens with grapes. In season, red and green grapes are plentiful and scrumptious. But the evolution of the standard sized 5-pound bag in my refrigerator involves stems turning brown, grapes getting sunken and soggy and then white fuzz growing on bottom-bag grapes. My whole grape dilemma changed when I spotted a store employee getting an empty bag off a roll and separating one grape bunch for their perfectly sized grape purchase. When I asked if that was legal, the response was "Of course! I if I brought home a 5-pound bag of grapes, my wife would kill me!" So there you have it: a grape solution and no more sour grapes. And you'll be glad to know this holds true for cherries, too.

And who can resist the grocery gals handing out samples of treats they just concocted on a toothpick? I'll never forget the day when I realized my life was not complete without chocolate hummus. You know hummus—that good-for-you spread made out of smashed chickpeas? Well it's now a dessert spread that tastes like the most delicious treat in the world. One cracker full of this and I was hooked. I believe this is the same approach that drug dealers use. The first is free, but then you're addicted and can't imagine life without it.

Another grocery store gotcha scheme is the two-fer. You know the one: two big jugs of juice fer $6. But I can only use one, so what to do? Unlike the BOGO, the two-fer easily converts to a one-fer. One big jug goes for $3 without any funny business. That is, until you remember that the last jug you bought was $2.75. It's best to just accept that grocery dealers are always one step ahead, and they are truly sorry you pushed a cart with a broken wheel for 3 miles around the aisles.

Lite Bites

Photos Finished?

Once upon a time, cameras were used to take photos on rolls of film. There was anticipation then joy when the roll was finally developed and prints were received, especially if the first picture was shot a long time ago. You could then review events in a mini time capsule of 12, 24 or 36 precious moments worth capturing and saving forever, even if some of those moments were out of focus or with someone's eyes closed. Good photos were then arranged in a book of sticky sheets or clear pockets, and the lucky pics were given captions or dates.

Of course, today things are drastically different. The "precious moments" captured on cell phones are as numerous as seconds in a day. So many shots are taken, so few actually viewed. Fewer still are carefully scrutinized, enhanced, printed and cherished for long periods of time. Printed photos? Many of today's teens have not held an actual photo in their hands. That's a tragedy on the scale of not learning to write cursive in school anymore, but I digress.

They say a picture is worth a thousand words, but many good photos also generate conversations of thousands of words, usually starting with *I remember when that was taken!* Call me old-fashioned, but there's nothing like flipping through the pages of a cherished album full of smiling faces and remembering the good times captured on 3x5-inch prints. Finger swipes on a cell screen just don't conjure up the same feelings.

Some folks are very photogenic, but it's safe to say that does not apply to anyone in my family. The remark most often heard is *Do I really look like that?* I'm not sure the proper way to answer that question, but assume it is *No, you look much better in real life.* But

- 20 -

yet, we still take them. The problem with photos of kids is that they're always in motion, so lots of blurred shots can get nixed right away. I've had success with sleeping baby photos, but then you miss out on the favorite baby-photo reaction of *Look at those big eyes!*

Posed photos in front of a landmark are good for a reference point, but there's always the one looking the wrong way or with the before-mentioned closed eyes. One of my friends has lots of photos taken long ago at family gatherings artfully framed and hung all over her house. Many people in the photos are no longer with us, so this is a way to keep them hanging around, so to speak.

I don't understand selfies, but I well understand selfie sticks. The ability to take a pic of you with quite a few other people eliminates the awkward camera swapping dance where the photo taker is never included, so you can't get a photo of the whole gang. The trick with the stick is to hold it high above everyone's heads so that you can fit more heads in the shot, and thankfully this angle also hides those awful under-chin sags and under-eye bags. The result is often picture perfect. But if not, everyone knows they look much better in real life.

Lite Bites

Lite Bites

Society's Quirks

Too Many Choices

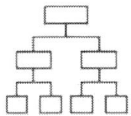 **We all like to have options,** but sometimes it's really annoying when you need to answer twenty questions to get something relatively common that should be uncomplicated to get. Take coffee, for instance. Regular or decaf is a good option, especially when ordering a cup of Joe when you just got out of bed or are planning to go there shortly. Black or with cream is another benign option, and the **answer doesn't require much thought.**

From there, it gets more complicated. Cappuccino? Café Au Lait? Frappuccino? Latte? Cream or skim milk? Or something non-dairy, maybe made from nuts or soy or something else? What flavor shot to add? Whipped cream on top? Mocha morsels? Maybe cinnamon?

One option that doesn't seem to exist anymore is *small*. Supersizing has hit the coffee market. The choices are tall, grandé, or a 55-gallon drum.

All of these decisions can take up your whole morning, so now it's time to hit a deli for lunch. White, wheat, rye, hoagie roll, ciabatta, or wrap? Lettuce, tomato, pickles and banana peppers maybe? Spicy mustard, yellow mustard, honey mustard, mayonnaise, lite mayo, oil and vinegar? Toasted, grilled or pressed?

I'm sure I heard of a scientist in a foreign country that determined that too many options caused the brain to become paralyzed. **Option overload just isn't good for a** person.

But it seems that some folks like to have all these options. "Which one of these 248 cell phone rings will best suit my personality and style and make the proper statement to my friends and co-workers?" "My mixed salad featuring seven leafy greens must be perfect, so I need to look through 84 dressings to choose just the right one." C'mon folks, can you really get 12 grains in one slice of bread?

To my way of thinking, choices are more often bad than good. When you call the water company to complain about your bill, you only want one choice: let me talk to a real human who has the understanding, willingness and authority to resolve my problem in the next five minutes. Instead, you get a choice of English or Spanish, followed by a decision tree that, if you go down the wrong branch, gets you on a mailing list for pamphlets with bar graphs of the levels of proclaimed non-toxic components of your drinking water.

But, we all know the phone trick: just scream *REPRESENTATIVE* and the option-chooser algorithm will connect you to a real human. Now that the entire free world knows this escape route, it's become less effective. You'll progress into a phone-hell queue, sometimes with an estimate of wait time, but always with maddening advertisements of how helpful your water company is, and what recent awards were bestowed on them for their superior customer service.

Maybe it's time to get back to the Life Savers' rule of choices. Just spiral peel the foil-covered paper to reveal the next flavor, and your only options are to eat it or give it to your brother.

Lite Bites

Battle of the Gases

Someone who makes gaseous products for a living has decided we all should fill our tires with nitrogen instead of air. The claimed benefits are numerous: better gas mileage, extending the life of your tires, decreasing the frequency your tires need to be pumped up and having your tires sport colorful green stem caps. I say that anyone who falls for that line probably failed high school chemistry and likely cheated their way through college marketing.

Air, if you recall from your early education, is made up of 78% nitrogen, 21% oxygen and 1% other gasses. So, back when everyone had black stem caps, we were 78% of the way to filling our tires with nitrogen. Now that you know you're only getting 22% of your money's worth, should you believe that small amount can make any difference?

Even without a refresher on molecular structure, you probably know the answer. So why is it that our neighbor made a quick U-turn into our driveway recently to excitedly announce that the gas station down the corner now offers nitrogen for just $2 per tire? After the 10-minute lecture delivered by my retired-chemist spouse with a pulsing pointed index finger, the gas station was going to have one less nitrogen customer, or at least one paying his $2 but with squinty eyes and a hearty dose of skepticism.

Such marketing ploys aren't limited to minor expenses for just nitrogen—some are much more costly and go the liquid route. Another neighbor had their perfectly functioning 3-year-old water heater and water softener ripped out and replaced with new ones that the salesman claimed would remove all the nasty stuff in the water that causes everything from hair loss to leg cramps to dental plaque. The sales pitch is done in the comfort of your home with a demonstration using your own drinking water. Toxins reveal themselves when a magic fluid delivered from an eye dropper turns a glass of your tap water a yucky brown. This demonstration puts the awestruck consumer on the path to *absolutely needing* different water processing, rather than wanting to know what the heck's in that eye dropper.

Then there's the neighbor with re-bent clothes hangers pointing skyward from their mounts on every peak on his rooftop. A pretty penny was shelled out so that these gizmos would make lightning bolts think twice before zapping his house. If they were bold enough to go that route, the hundred-million volts would be swished away to the ground so that the home and all its electronic components would survive unscathed.

This approach reminds me of the hex signs on Pennsylvania Dutch farm houses, except they were decorative, inexpensive, and the owners didn't *really* believe that they would influence their lives for the better.

It was in the 1800s when somebody said, "There's a sucker born every minute," questionably attributed to huckster P. T. Barnum. Our population has increased six times since then, while the number of things we need protection from has exploded with the digital age (No, sir. I don't believe I inherited 30 million dollars from a Nigerian prince.)

I hope my suspicious nature will last the length of my purchasing power so I'm never a victim of one of those scams targeting the elderly. But since green is my favorite color, I still might grab a few colorful tire valve caps someday when they no longer signal a sucker for nitrogen.

Lite Bites

Running Behind

As if highway travel wasn't filled with enough stress, why is it that I get smack behind the garbage truck more than one day a week on my commute to work? Trailing behind a waste-management load is fraught with challenges—the most notable being that unmistakable odor. If you're stuck in the wake of the smell, there is no amount of window opening or air-conditioning settings that provide relief.

Another trash-truck-tailing problem is the dropping of said trash. Sometimes it's solid, other times it's liquid, and I've actually seen a skanky mixture of both. In all cases, it's nothing that you'd ever want plopped or dribbled on your car or even on the pavement you're driving your car on.

Even another hazard of following a dump-delivery vehicle is that it obscures from vision all things in front of it. As it slows down to a stop, you are left to wonder if there's a traffic jam or the driver is just taking a time out.

Once the stop is over, then comes the really, really long wait to start up again. Fifteen or so gear shifts later, the trash load gets just about up to the speed limit, usually in time to be positioned in front of another stop light turning red. For multi-lane roads, having the traffic to your left and right move far ahead of you at slightly above the speed limit only makes a bad situation worse.

To cope with this problem, I try to think of what life would be like without trash removal. In no time, we'd be shoulder high in all kinds of stuff that we never wanted to see again, while learning how bad food can smell when it smelled so good just a few days prior.

I also think about those who do trash removal being out of a job. I'm not sure what motivates them, but the trash collectors in our neighborhood actually *run* to and from the truck and lob pretty sizable bags of junk into the back of the trucks from fair distances. Are they training for some athletic or future Olympic event that rewards moving at breakneck speeds and hurling heavy bags farther than anyone else? Or are they moving as fast as they can so they'll be done sooner? It seems their workday is over when the curbs are cleared of rubbish. It's not like the boss is going to make them just hang around if no more bags need to be tossed. In any event, I'm sure grateful to those folks who list *trash collector* as their chosen occupation.

So the next time I'm detained in traffic by a large load of lumbering litter, I'll be happy that I'm not behind the gal putting on her makeup or the guy texting his buddy. They're the ones that can really trash your day in a hurry.

A Word from our Sponsors

Except during the Super Bowl, commercial breaks are the universal cue to get off the couch and go to the kitchen or bathroom, depending on the urge of the moment. Switching to another channel to avoid ads just doesn't work. This is because all broadcast channels across the planet have a secret pact to perfectly synchronize the start of commercials. While I understand the need for paid advertising, I have to say the sponsors aren't getting their money's worth at my house.

Including a pet in an insurance commercial is a detractor to the 0.04% of households (mine and three others) that don't have a pet and never ever will have a pet. Informing us of a new drug with a name that includes Xs and Zs and not many vowels to cure an ailment that's equally unpronounceable won't motivate us to talk with our doctor.

While our memories may not be as sharp as they once were, something in a bottle won't be the sharpening stone to cut through brain fog. And, for the record, it's not a bad thing to print out directions when you're traveling to an unknown location when it's important you arrive on time. More than once, stormy skies blocked my GPS signal, and I was very happy I had my print-out that clearly listed my go-lefts, continue-straights, and go-rights.

In case you wonder about such things, there are at least eight minutes of commercials during a 30-minute show. You will not be surprised that most of the commercial break is toward the end of the program so you'll hang in there for more than a few minutes wondering about the show's wrap-up or the newsy feel-good story.

"What was that an ad for?" is a common question in my house. We just *don't get* some commercials, and that's fine since we're not the target audience. Although we're in the upper end of the age groups, we're not in the lower end of the intelligence groups, and some commercials may rub an intelligent mature audience the wrong way.

In all fairness, there are a few ads that we find entertaining or motivating enough to go and check out the product. Some commercials with steaming food, crisp veggies, or smothering sauce sliding in slow-motion can initiate a salivary reflex and a search for the nearest place where we can compare the actual taste to the visuals.

New car commercials grab our attention. We always want to know if next year's sports car looks like the last year's or maybe there was a design overhaul. Do you know why car ads must admit there a professional driver at the wheel laying rubber through hairpin turns or kicking up large plumes of dust in the dessert? I don't either. Oftentimes, a new car ad shows interaction with a professional actor and it knows what kind of music to play and just the right ambient lighting. Cars are no longer just for transportation, but after 30 seconds of imagining the new car in *our* garage, we're on to another commercial.

Is it possible to watch regular TV for 30 minutes without any commercial interruptions? Yes, but they're called infomercials—very long sales pitches with zero interruptions. How great is that?

Gated Communities

There are an awful lot of gated communities in the state of Florida, and they all have one thing in common: the gate is usually broken. A gate's purpose is to let good neighbors in and keep the boogeyman out. Community brochures claim the security offered by a gated community is well worth the chunk of those association fees you'll pay for upkeep and continuous repair of the gate. When you actually see those charges on a community's balance sheet, the gratuity for the gate is not so great.

Entry gates are typically a two-part system: the metalwork doors that are the preamble to entry. These move painfully slow, accompanied by requisite creaking sounds, and they need to come to a full-open position before the second part, a plastic sacrificial striped barrier arm, pivots from horizontal to vertical. The striped barrier arm is sacrificial because that's the piece that all-too-often gets whacked by too-fast drivers unwilling to wait for the vertical position or too-slow drivers pausing in the path of the arm rotating from vertical to horizontal. When the sacrificial arm gets damaged, the metal doors are smart enough to stay out of the way and stick wide open, where they patiently wait days and sometimes weeks for the arm to get repaired.

Arm damage happens so frequently that our community installed cameras to get live action of the vehicle causing the damage. Community employees scan the video and zoom in on the license plate of the offending vehicle. Then the process starts of finding the owner, presenting them with a repair bill, following up to make sure they paid up, and so on. Costs for security cameras and gumshoeing were also captured on our community's balance sheet but are probably buried under a non-related category.

It was our neighbors at the top of the alphabetical name list that infrequent guests bothered when seeking entry. They would get gate calls at all times of the day and night from visitors without proper entry instructions: pizza distribution kids who didn't know who ordered what, delivery trucks from appliance stores, and sometimes, fire-rescue folks who weren't given the secret code for 'open sesame.' Those were the guys who firmly and loudly announced their arrival with a demand to get the gate open, pronto. Not once did the boogeyman ask for entry.

Gated-community residents are usually offered a remote control device for the entry gate—a swell idea when it's pouring rain. You don't have to stick your arm outside to the keypad and punch in numbers. For a handsome sum, you stay dry inside your vehicle and command the gate to open. The remote worked great except during rainstorms when the signal gets dampened to the point of being ineffective.

We have lived in both gated and non-gated communities and there are pros and cons of each. In the end, perhaps the only gates I really care about entering are the Pearly ones. If I get there, I sure hope I can tailgate and get in behind the person ahead of me before the goddamn plastic arm comes down.

Lite Bites

The Best Superpower

One good way to start a conversation with a kid is to ask what superpower they'd wish for. The ability to fly may be the most popular answer. Perhaps landing safely after flight is assumed, but I'd be specific on that point if responding to a genie out of a bottle. If the genie asked *me* that question, my answer would be the ability to know the precise words to evoke the reaction I desired. Why not? It happens all the time in movies, just like other superpowers. Rhett Butler's "Frankly, my dear, I don't give a damn" caused Scarlett and zillions of viewers to gasp. The Terminator's "I'll be back" moved all of us fast forward to the next sequel.

But honestly, wouldn't it be great to find the exact words that would transform a sobbing child into a giggling one? How about making a bad guy re-think the mischief he was about to do? *Go ahead, make my day.* I'm not one for long conversations, so how about a few phrases that would make the check-out kid at the grocery store stop tossing heavy frozen stuff on top of my smooth, ripe, yellow bananas. When this happens the unbagging process reveals brown lines and dents on the previously picture-perfect fruit I chose.

We all know the thought-provoking clichés attributed to famous thinkers. Mark Twain is credited with the wisely witty "I've had a lot of worries in my life, most of which never happened." The phrase makes people grin, then hopefully snap out of ruminating over stuff in the past that really wasn't so bad. During my career I picked up the 5-year rule. One engineer was struggling with missing his daughter's much-anticipated birthday party to attend an important business meeting out of town. When I asked him which event would be more important to him 5 years from now, he cancelled his flights.

The good thing about **superpowers** is that they're typically used for making the world a better place. Kids want to fly so they can rescue people from danger. Our beloved superheroes battle villains daily to save the family, the town, the country, or the planet from harm. Characters develop and we all clap at the happy ending. Superpowers are fun.

So, if I were granted the superpower of words it would have to go way deeper than the daily grind. Perhaps I could choose words that are cherished for a long time, or **could improve someone's** outlook, or help with a key life decision. My sweetie claims that when he was thinking about retirement, my question to him flipped the decision switch.

After working very hard for very many years, he felt he should work just a bit **longer to build a slightly bigger nest egg.** "What would you do differently during retirement if you had twice the **money in the bank?" was all I had to say to make him start filling out the retirement paperwork.** I've received thanks for that line dozens of times over the years. Hey—maybe I do have that superpower after all!

Lite Bites

The Lullaby of Broadway

No, I don't mind people talking and then suddenly breaking into song. Especially when they're talented actors and are performing *Cabaret*. However I know there are a lot of folks who just don't like musicals. "People don't just start singing in the real world," they say. Well, people don't project their voices into the audience and have their apartment furniture on a stage in the real world either! It's entertainment and not meant to be the real world. We get enough of the real world being in the real world, don't we?

So, if you're like me and love musicals, we can now move on to discuss our favorites. I'm leaning toward the classics since they're usually happy (notable exceptions are *Les Misérables* and *The Phantom of the Opera*) and there's nothing like catchy music sung by beautiful voices. My first musical was *Mary Poppins* seen at a drive-in with my parents. I fell asleep, but I was about four years old, so I think that's forgivable. I made up for it by watching the whole show on TV and staying awake every time until the end. Julie Andrews' voice was mesmerizing, which is why my next memorable musical was *The Sound of Music*. All those kids harmonizing perfectly after just one practice round of *Do-Re-Mi* was miraculous. But *My Fair Lady* takes the cake for music—singing *I Could Have Danced all Night* with an English accent is *Loverly* and warms the cockles of your heart.

I have been lucky enough to see Broadway performances of *A Chorus Line* and *CATS*. *A Chorus Line* was special because it was a musical about auditions for a musical. The finale showcasing a long line of dancers in super shiny silver outfits with perfectly synchronous kicks is a scene that will stick with you forever. *CATS* started out special with the whole theater 'decorated' with outsized trash so the ratio of you to the trash was equal to the ratio of a cat to regular-sized trash. Set designers are awesome.

Not everyone owned an eight-track tape of ABBA back in the day, but anyone who heard their songs has gotta like *Momma Mia*, the story about three dads that weaves a bit of dialogue around 18 ABBA songs that you can't **believe** you remember all the words to.

But there's a reason why the classics are so classic. *OOOOklahoma, where the wind comes sweepin' down the plain.* I've heard it dozens of times, and in my head I still sing *Oh, What a Beautiful Mornin'* on bright sunny mornings that portend a good day. *42nd Street* first hit the scene in 1933, but it's *The Lullaby of Broadway* just as much now as it was then.

More recent musicals can feature animated characters that get *Frozen* inside your head. Idina Menzel actually apologized to millions of moms who listened millions of times to her belting out the rising riffs of *Let It Go* while their kids watched the movie over and over and over.

But that's what musicals do—they draw you in, so you spend some time in a fantasy world where people are perfectly dressed and perfectly choreographed and belt out songs in the middle of dialogue.

Too bad the real world isn't like that.

Pick Me!

Any well-considered advice on how to spend gratifying time during the 4th quarter of your life will include a *very strong* suggestion to volunteer. The benefits of volunteering read like those of eating well and exercising: it keeps the brain active, improves your quality of life, strengthens social networks, and lowers mortality rates. I don't know why eating cheesecake for dessert every day can't also yield these benefits, but maybe someday it will.

The essence of volunteering is to perform duties under someone's direction without pay. If you get paid that's called *work*, and that's what many of us do most of our lives. If you had a good career and save properly, then you are able to share some of your time and effort without compensation. But you really *do* get rewarded with the above-mentioned bennies, and they aren't dollars so they don't make your tax forms more difficult.

I am proud to say that I'm a volunteer, and quietly admit that the benefits, other than those listed above, far outweigh the effort. The hardest part in figuring out how to volunteer was choosing the duties I'd be willing to perform for free. One of the first places I checked was AARP's volunteer option survey. After all, they have *Retired* in their name and I figured it would be a snap to zero in on the perfect faux job. They even included virtual volunteering (VV)—something you can do from home, which makes sense because a lot of folks now handle real work at home. Don't think there are only a few virtual volunteer options out there; AARP lists the VVs alphabetically on their website and it takes lots of scrolling to go from top to bottom of the list. So, the choice of volunteering activity may be as complex as the choice of jobs, but that shouldn't dismay you.

There's no free lunch. We all heard that before, but I'm here to say it's not true, and lunch was delicious. You see, organizations feel that since you're volunteering (and not getting paid), you should be thanked in some manner that avoids legal tender. Sometimes it's food, sometimes it's merchandise, sometimes it's tickets to the theater. Whatever it is, it's all good. A friend of mine shows patrons to their seats at the theater. In return, she gets tickets to performances. She periodically hosts a theater night, which is enjoyed by a whole gaggle of gals. I'll bet her besties treat her to a drink or special gift in return, and that keeps the whole circle of giving twirling around.

One really special feature of volunteering is that you likely won't get fired. The word *likely* is used here because every earthly organization has rules and regulations that must be followed. Going in with the attitude that you'll help out only on your own terms is not going to sit well with the Director of Volunteers, and you may be the first to get your volunteer ass fired. Don't do that.

So, the next time you're thinking about charitably giving of your time, you can rest assured that if you follow the rules your efforts may be acknowledged in a lot of ways, some more tangible than an improved quality of your life. Just maybe your organization will treat you to cheesecake for dessert.

Lite Bites

License and Registration

If you've never heard a request from the police to see your license and registration, you live a very lucky life or always drive within the speed limit. Even though I consider myself very lucky, I have to admit I've heard this request numerous times and in numerous states. It started on Pennsylvania highways when I was pulled over a few times and given a warning to ease off on the gas. "Yes, sir. Will do."

Three days after I moved to New York State, I was pulled over on a side street doing 50mph in a 35mph zone. I humbly confessed I was new in town, and Pennsylvania police just over the state boarder only checked your speed when you were on a highway. The nice cop kindly explained the law to me when he realized I was honestly amazed by the situation after my half-baked explanation, which also included my erroneous assumption that radar guns don't operate below 50mph.

The number of times I was requested to produce my license and registration got to the point that I had to go to safe-driving school to avoid loading more points on my license and face sky-high insurance rates. Back then, safe driving school could be done in person or on line. One on-line class was advertised as an *Improv* version. I really wish I picked that one to know how safe driving could be amusing. The in-person one I picked was in an unfamiliar part of town, so of course I got lost on my way and was 10 minutes late for class. When I arrived, and thinking of the *improv* class I could be watching at home, I joked to the instructor—and the class I disrupted—that I would have arrived on time but got stopped for speeding. Believe me when I say that not all save-driving instructors have a sense of humor.

One license-and-registration incident occurred on a rainy night in Florida on a side street, admittedly in a speed trap. I knew it was a speed trap because the very nice police officer told me the speed limit changed from 45mph to 30mph right after the bridge, "and a lot of people don't realize that 'cause the sign is hidden behind the tree." "No sir. I didn't realize that at all, but I'll be sure to pay real close attention in the future," I replied with fervent head shaking and nodding at the appropriate times. I got away with a warning on that one.

Another warning was issued when I was pulled over on my way to work at 6am. The officer took my license and registration and sat in his car for a really long time. He then returned and explained it was hard for him to accept that a woman ***of my age*** was driving so fast. But it was the end of his shift. And he was feeling generous. So he would let me off with just a warning. I drove away wondering how I got so old and since when did they allow 12-year-olds to work as police officers? I think that just this one time, I would rather have gotten a ticket.

Lite Bites

About Face

My college boyfriend casually mentioned that he thought I had a big nose. I hadn't thought once about my nose before he said that, but I thought about it a million times afterward. Mostly about how big it was and how I hadn't noticed it before. Since college, no one mentioned my nose again, so maybe it's not so bad after all. But you can't ignore all the attention noses get, and all of it is deserved.

Not only is the nose the centerpiece of your face, it can do a lot of marvelous things. It can run. And that's marvelous only because the legs are so far away. It should not be pointed in the air, which gives the impression of snobbishness. Keeping your nose clean is important for a lot of reasons, as well as the literal one. If a measurement is *on the nose*, it's precise—*one o'clock on the nose*.

It's easy to stick your nose where it doesn't belong. And when you do, it's likely someone will rub your nose in it to remind you about the intrusion. So just keep your nose to the grindstone and good fortune will spring up right under your nose.

The medical community and moms everywhere depend on noses quite a bit for diagnoses. The sniffles call for a bowl of chicken soup, or a warm embrace when tearing eyes join the sniffles. The nose is the runway to the sinuses when investigating allergies or infections.

While the ears have specially designed cotton swabs for periodic cleaning, swabs are confined to the bathroom. You can note that *powdering one's nose* is the gracious way of excusing yourself to that swab-containing room. Unlike swabs, nose-clearing tissues are ubiquitous since you'll never know when the need will arise.

The nose has powers that other body parts are grateful for. It acts as quality control for milk and other food to make sure only good-smelling stuff gets passed on to the taste buds. It can sniff out a rat to avoid an ache to the heart. It's the first warning signal when dinner is left in the oven too long. And it teams quite well with the ears to make an effective location for eyeglasses to set. If someone tells you that your feet smell, well, you can call out their error and correctly point out that's the job for the nose.

Speaking of nose jobs, there are a lot of actors that decided to tweak what Mother Nature gave them, and that provides us a lot of before-and-after photos. But some famous folk embrace their prominent proboscises. Comedian Jimmy Durante became famous with his self-depreciating humor involving his schnozzola. Bob Hope's ski-slope-shaped nose is immortalized in his famous caricature drawing. Barbara Streisand, despite a lot of encouragement, refused a touch-up because it might affect her singing voice. We all thank you, Ms. Streisand. And who can forget Pinocchio, with a nose growing longer with each lie.

The most interesting and powerful nose activity must be that of Elizabeth Montgomery's Bewitched character, Samantha Stephens, who was able to twitch her nose to make magic happen. Samantha owned the magic, but Elizabeth mastered the twitch. I'm sure little girls everywhere (me included) tried many times to replicate that twitch. If we had only known the nose doesn't have muscles that make it wiggle. Samantha's nose twitch was actually an illusion created by moving her lips back and forth. Think of it as the origin of special affects without digital intervention.

Lite Bites

One of the most admired faces that carry an often-talked-about nose is that of the Mona Lisa. While her face may be best known for her mysterious smile, she is said to have a Greek nose—straight and strong. I'll bet Leonardo da Vinci never told Lisa her nose was big.

Lite Bites

Aging Affects the Young

Waist Not, Why Not?

Once upon a time, I had a waist. One that was fewer inches in circumference than my bust and my hips. But now it's gone. My middle section should be identified by my torso going in, but now I need my belly button for a reference point where a shapely figure should be shaped. A friend's doctor says it's the body's way of protecting your pancreas with a layer of padding. I guess my body was focused on attracting a mate in my younger days, but now it's worried about my organs.

There's a boatload of reasons why my waist is nowhere to be found: hormone hell, mid-life vengeance, fat cells' preference for the center-of-gravity district, a dawdling metabolism. Paid advertising offers just as many fixes for the problem: Pilates, pills, an ab-ercizer and various paunch-be-gone gizmos that fold to fit under the bed.

Along with the bags and sags of middle age comes the mass migration. Although your weight may be within ounces of what it was on graduation day, Mother Nature redistributed it to make a lovingly described *muffin top*, the fleshy part hanging over the waistband.

And speaking of waistbands, why do pants styles have a waistband at the exact location of the lower belly bulge? It's a *waistband*, for Pete's sake. Trying on these pants in the harsh glare of the fitting rooms without anything to hide the pinched-in paunch is a self-realization moment akin to trying on swimsuits in January. Bring back high-waist pants and don't ever let them go out of style again, please.

In my latest hunt for a pair of pants that fit, the same number of slacks that I took into the dressing room was returned to the lady that gave me the hang tag with the number nine on it. She asked the women exiting in front of me if she found something she could use, to which the lady replied, "I found that I need to stop eating."

I've been hoping that scientists will have a revelation about good fat and bad fat. They did it before. Remember the earth-shattering news about good cholesterol and bad cholesterol? Unfortunately, the latest theory is that there are two types of fat. There's bad fat and then there's downright evil fat. Evil fat is called visceral fat, and it lives—you got it—right around your middle. It's the kind of fat that taunts your heart to clog up and stop functioning. Pure evil.

No quantity of sit-ups will decrease your visceral fat. You must follow the same directions given by the medical community for living longer and being healthy: exercise and eat right. Choosing a set of parents that don't have a propensity for around-the-waist fat is also a good idea, but that's as easy as exercising and eating right.

There's also the advice given by the fashion community: wear a brightly colored scarf around your neck and no one will notice the spare tire a foot below it. If all apple-shaped women just bought up and wore the earth's supply of brightly colored scarfs, would this problem go away? Perhaps not.

I really do miss my waist, and I don't know that I'll ever see it again. As it goes with the yin and yang of life, whenever you lose something, you also gain something. In my case, when I lost my waist, I gained another chin. It's just not fair.

A Fondness for Memories

As our population ages, there's more news about the annoyance of memory loss. The truth of the matter is that the memories are intact—it's the search engine that's gone kaput. How many times have you awakened at 3 a.m. and thought of the actor's name that escaped you earlier during two hours of dinner conversation with your friends? His name was there all the time; it's just that retrieval took five hours rather than two seconds. Things just take longer when you age. You can't run as fast as you could in high school, can you?

Instead of stressing about this condition, it forces you to develop other skills much more useful than remembering actors' names. One such skill is discussing a person whose name you can't remember without looking like an idiot. Those growing old can engage gracefully in lively discussions without populating it with items that were once important—like people's names. They do this without saying "Just give me a second" while grimacing and slapping their forehead in an attempt to make the brain's data fetcher get into gear. These folks just get over it, realize that the name they're seeking may be on an eight-hour delay, and then get on with the story.

If it's any consolation, computers fail the same way. As their hard drives get packed with a bunch of useless and little-used data, it gets harder to get to the important stuff. Microsoft had a little fetch doggie Rover (shown above) that provided amusement while searching. It helped if you had some notion of what the doggie can dig up. I used this doggie quite a bit back in the day, but many times he tires, and then puts on a sad face when he comes up with nothing. I've chalked this up to giving poor doggie commands.

If the name you're seeking is germane to the story being told—like the one that starts: "*Guess who I ran into the other day?*" sometimes it's fun to go through a game of talking charades to try to elicit the name from others involved in the conversation, but make sure there is one clue given for each wrong try.

"You know who I mean; he's tall and wears glasses."
"Ed?"
"No, he's shorter than Ed and drove a sporty red car."
"Bill?"
"Not Bill, but he hung around with Bill. You're getting close!"

Perhaps more fun than retrieval-challenged memory games are the recollections that have transformed with the passage of time. Fishing anecdotes offer the best analogy. The big one that got away will grow an inch for every year the story is told. I've been hearing tall tales for more than two decades, and have listened to the fish that got away morph from being a good size to one that nearly sank the boat. Crowd sizes grow larger over time as do distances travelled. We've all heard our elders lament how they walked five miles to school each day, uphill both ways.

But the most interesting memories are those that never happened. I've heard a good friend recount a funny situation that he remembered happened to him as a kid. He said it so many times that recently another friend told the same story as if it were his own. Mark Twain sums it up best when he said, "When I was younger I could remember anything, whether it happened or not."

Lite Bites

Two Piece or Not Two Piece

Once upon a time, I wore two-piece bathing suites. I had both a waist and a flat stomach. I probably looked OK. But today—well, not so much. Skin is blotchy and saggy. Bingo wings hang from the backs of arms. There's bra bulge. Some saddle bags. Don't forget muffin tops. Cankles are the blending of calves and ankles. Thuts are a merger of the thigh and butt. So many names for so many new body parts. Not one is welcome.

Absurd things happen during aging and you're left pretty much helpless. The area below the bra line and above the belly button starts to protrude. Taut skin turns into what's known as crepey skin because its appearance is 'finely wrinkled like crepe paper.' Remember the brightly colored sagging streamers hanging from ceilings to decorate birthday celebrations? That same surface eventually decorates necks, arms and legs. Now everyone yell *Surprise*!

We learn the cause of crepey skin is the loss of collagen and elastin. This is due to the excess of sun exposure and aging. These two factors are equally impossible to avoid. To conquer crepey skin, treatments include a plethora of chemical, laser, ultrasound, scrubbing, acid, freezing and filling procedures. Call me doubtful, but I'm sure some of these solutions may only serve to fill a clinic's bank account.

Not only does skin terrain become un-smooth, it also becomes un-clear. Sun spots should be in the skies, not on thighs. Irish freckles, once adorably known as angle's kisses, morph into something that makes dermatologists grimace and grab liquid nitrogen to burn off. And speaking of doctors, by this stage of life it's not unlikely that a surgeon has cut something *out of* or *off of* your body leaving behind a permanent reminder of the incident. That's probably another thing you don't want to be a conversation starter with a stranger at the pool.

So with all these crinkles, sags, spots and scars, how do you confidently wear a two-piece swim suit in public? Fortunately, bathing suit designers are making clothes out of swimsuit material and telling us to wear these newfangled pieces by the water. A rash guard is said to have originated from surfers that wanted to protect their skin from the board. I don't think so. It's just a long-sleeve, high-neck tee that covers all you want it to. Perfect! Board shorts and swim skirts are just as they sound, but with material that dries quickly and hides all that should be kept from the light of day. There are even swim dresses that overtly cover all that hangs between your shoulders and your knees. Brilliant!

But wait—is any of this new? Of course not. Just add stockings and a hat and we're now wearing swim suits ladies wore in the early 1900s. That's more than 100 years ago and validates the saying that everything old is new again.

It was 1946 when the skimpy two-piece suit was introduced. It was named after the little Bikini Atoll where the U.S. detonated some nuclear bombs. Not sure of the connection there, but a search for a person to model the bikini ended when a nude dancer agreed to be the first one to show it off—or maybe she was putting her own assets on display.

I'll be wearing a more modest swimsuit when I see you by the pool or at the beach. And I may get comfortable enough in the water to slide my long sleeves up a bit.

Lite Bites

Coming of Age

Everyone remembers times in their childhood where they felt scared, out-of-place, different from normal, unable to make friends or just weird. Some of us felt that way all through childhood. My best friend and I lived in a small town with lots of culm dumps—mountains of burning coal mine waste that glowed red at night and belched noxious sulfur fumes when it rained. Our whole world was made up of family, neighbors, teachers and each other. Everyone else outside this dozen-person circle was a stranger and, therefore, to be feared.

So, imagine our terror when my best friend and I visited my sister and her husband at their lake cottage one summer and were told to walk over to the neighbor's house and play with the group of kids who gathered there on the weekends. This was at night, when it was dark, in unfamiliar woods, with strange kids and no adults.

My best friend and I should have been thrilled to meet new kids our age and see what lake-cottage kids do to have fun at night. However, as young teens with the emotional maturity of third graders, we picked our way through the woods hoping we wouldn't step on any snakes and trying not to wet our pants.

How many kids were going to be there? What if they were smoking? How about if they were drinking? Were they going to have knives? Were they playing with guns? Or is it possible they were doing something worse or wanted to do something worse with us? Or *to* us? How deep is this lake anyhow and how long would it take police to find our bodies? What we lacked in maturity, we more than made up for with our bizarre imaginations.

I don't remember how long it took before we got the nerve to knock on the door, but we did, and announced we were visiting the neighbors down the block and came there to hang out for a while. That was likely the bravest thing we've done in our lives up to that point, and for a long time afterwards for that matter.

We were welcomed inside and told the names of a bunch of kids who looked like they were left alone a lot and maybe weren't required to bathe every day. We presumed their parents gathered at another cottage to spend time with the adults, and these kids were left to entertain themselves, which they did very easily given a canoe and a deck of cards. We learned a card game that involved spitting or sticking your tongue out—don't remember which. When tired of that, our gang took canoe rides then wandered around the lake looking for bats or worms or some other creatures they were after. They all yelled and screamed at each other about where they were or what they found. There was no scary music in the background and I didn't see any chainsaws, so big relief there.

After some bug bites and branch-scratched legs, my friend and I decided it was time to go back to my sister's place, but we didn't know how to find it in the dark. The kids were gracious enough to gather up some flashlights and take us back, but it took a lot longer to return than the trip over there, and that caused another wave of panic, just as unfounded as previous ones.

In the end, we had a pleasant evening with new-found friends and a lot of needless worry. But that was simply in our DNA and was to continue throughout our lives. We put more effort into making up scenarios about what could go wrong while missing out enjoying the present. I attribute our nature to something eking out of those old culm dumps all around our hometown.

Lite Bites

Mattresses' Sinking Feeling

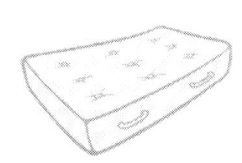

The year was 2007, or thereabouts. That's when major mattress manufacturers eradicated the two-sided mattress. This tragic point in our history may have been good for mattress makers, but I think anyone who sleeps thought it was a change for the worse.

Back in the day, ovens, refrigerators, washers, dryers, and mattresses were replaced only after a decade or two of use. The lifespan of a mattress depended on frequent rotations and flips. The bonus with a king mattress was that you can get four rotational positions, while queens and singles would give you two. But then you would flip the mattress over and double the locations where your head would lay. And it worked! You really felt better the morning after sleeping on a freshly flipped or twirled mattress.

Then came the commercials about dust mites and allergens building up to a level after only eight years that your mattress would weigh twice as much as when new. When you thought about that claim, it was obviously hogwash, but it grossed everyone out and they ran to get a new mattress. It was supremely effective advertising.

But that new mattress would likely survive less than a year before **hammock valleys were noticeable. And that's when you realized or remembered you couldn't flip it. Few buyers focused on this** during the purchase phase—why would you? You and your bed partner lay on a bunch of mattresses in the store and picked out one with the best comfort and cost compromise. Next was just haggling about the delivery charge and whether they would take the old, mite-infested mattress away with them. The reality that you were buying half a mattress **didn't really sink in, and sales** folks had that tidbit cozily tucked away. If you were aware of the no-flipping-allowed design, you were likely told that the new-age materials would make them last as long as your two-sided beds of old. More hogwash, I say to that.

So there you are, with your open-faced-sandwich of a mattress with noticeable sunken areas and no recourse. "Nothing changes for the better," my wise friend Jim says, and he hit the nail on the headboard in this case. You twirl the mattress for a few years until the morning achiness can't be ignored, then it's on your way to buy a new mattress that won't sag. Which ones won't sag? Well, the ones that cost more than the last one you bought.

The good news is that more companies now realize there's a market and revenue opportunity to sell a flippable mattress, but most feature a different firmness level between the two sides. I don't know that I fully understand that twisted rationale, but I do know that when I'm in the market again, I'll likely give a two-sided version the nod. I want to lay my head in as many locations on that new mattress as possible. And I'll be able to manage flipping it since it won't be doubling its weight due to dust mites.

Lite Bites

Find a Penny

"See a penny, pick it up." With full realization of the true value of a penny, I still bend over to pick up any shiny coin I spy on the ground. The saying goes that if you make the effort to snatch the penny, "all day long you'll have good luck." But with every rule, there's the caveat. The caveat here is that you'll only get good luck if the penny is head's up. Head's down indicates the flip side—something is bound to go wrong. The simple solution to the bad-luck scenario is to flip the coin over so the next person can reap good luck. Bad fate averted!

No one can really pinpoint when that find-a-penny phrase was coined, but a little imagination leads you to believe that any money you come across is bound to be a good thing. But maybe that was before 2005 when it actually cost less than a penny to mint a penny. Nowadays it costs almost 2 cents to make that copper-colored coin, which is about 97% zinc since copper costs too much. So a penny comes into this world almost a penny in debt. But the old saying about finding a penny continues with, "…give it to a faithful friend, then your luck will never end." So, this old saying is actually a teaching moment, but just what can that friend do with the penny?

You can't get penny candy for a penny anymore, but it's good to know that a penny is still the going rate for your thoughts. However, if you ask someone to make that trade you'll get a blank stare and the "nothin" reply, which may mean their thoughts weren't even worth a penny. That thoughtless person may just be the bad penny we hear about. How about penny stocks? Well, 'penny' in stock jargon is just another way to say 'cheap.' Apple was once considered a penny stock, but that was when it was under $8 a share and well before everyone had a cell phone carrying its logo. Now, the Apple marketers dismiss the sky-high price of their ubiquitous cell phone and claim that Android users are just being penny wise and pound foolish.

If you're not a spendthrift, you may be a penny pincher. I have Scottish in my lineage and I understand they have been characterized as penny-pinchers. I do resemble this characterization since I'm picking up all this tossed coinage, but I'd prefer to think that saving and spending your hard-earned pennies wisely is a sign of fiscal maturity.

You have to wonder: since no one carries change anymore, where do those pennies on the ground come from? The correct answer is Heaven. We know this from that popular 1930s song. Angels up there are pitching pennies down here to show they're crossing your path, and their intent is to bring you comfort. Souls who have gone ahead don't want to startle you with a big ball of fire to say *Hi*, so they put a penny in your path to give you pause and let you know that everything will be OK.

Now that you know the truth, I'll bet you can't pass by the next penny without stooping over and doing what's proper.

Lite Bites

Game Time

While growing up, one of my favorite board games was Scrabble. I played it a lot with my mother, but she was much better at wordology, or maybe she just had really good luck picking usable letters. Now I'm an unabashed homebody at a stage of life when I'm quite fond of board-game dates with friends, and Scrabble is still my favorite. Some folks just don't Scrabble very well, but it seems that everyone is willing to give it a try. It's a good way to spend an evening, but you gotta have the dictionary!

When my friend Marion and I made our first Scrabble date, I jokingly asked her if she had the *official* dictionary. To my surprise, she confirmed that she indeed had one, sent me a photo of her genuine Merriam-Webster Official SCRABBLE Players Dictionary, and apologized for its advanced age. Then I figured I was in for a wicked word whipping. It turns out we were pretty evenly matched, but I lost because she used all her tiles, and I was left with that damn "Q" for which I had to deduct 10 points. That 10-point deduction put my score below hers. Of course, she picked all the "U" tiles, so my loss on this one was unarguably due to bad luck.

You learn a lot about people when playing Scrabble. You can also learn a lot about yourself. I put down letters that made a real word in my head, and I got challenged. My friend Barb, who is the most generous and honest person I know, clicked her tongue and shook her head. I grabbed for the official dictionary, and lo and behold she was correct—my letters didn't make a word. I chalk it up to the pressure of trying to make a word having four "O" tiles to deal with.

Scrabble was developed back in the 1930s by an architect named Butts. *Butts* is an official word in the Scrabble dictionary and can

- 58 -

earn you 21 points if you land it on a triple-word spot, which is my laser focus when playing. *Scrabble* is also an official word that refers to groping about frantically. If you're lucky enough to use that eight-letter word, you'll get a bonus 50 points because you'll be using all seven tiles. Sweet!

According to unofficial records, Scrabble burst onto the popular scene in the 1950s, when the president of Macy's became hooked while vacationing and started selling the game in his stores. The popularity of Scrabble grew steadily, and Macy's couldn't keep enough in stock.

Fast forward to today. You should not be surprised that a North American Scrabble Players Association hosts a yearly national championship. Hundreds of wordy, competitive types play for five days, and the winner takes home a sizable check. Certainly, it's a small fraction of what poker champions win, but Scrabble doesn't lend itself to the same profitable TV coverage because the contestants don't toss jabs at each other about bluffing. Also, today's poker algorithms can let you know the probability of someone winning when they peek at their first cards, causing you to cringe when the obvious loser pushes all their chips into the pot.

So, we owe the enjoyment of Scrabble to Mr. Butts. Legend has it that Butts used the front page of *The New York Times* to make his calculations for the distribution of game letters, and the point value of each letter. I just wish he made "Q" worth fewer points so I coulda won that game with Marion.

Lite Bites

Raising a Green Thumb

If the image you conjure up for gardening is a mature woman in a straw hat with an artfully decorated watering can sprinkling dozens of beautiful blooms around the sunny perimeter of her house, well then you never got your hands dirty, have you? A gardener is someone caring for living things to give them a long and healthy life, and depending on the circumstance, is a blend of a pediatrician and mortician. You see a lot of beautiful budding life, but you also see a lot at the other end of the gamut. For those of us not born with a green thumb but wanting to successfully foster our favorite flora in pots, there is something we absolutely need, and that is *technology.* Let me explain.

My dear friend gave me a shamrock plant for St. Patrick's Day. It was the perfect gift on one of my favorite days. It had big, green clovers and lots of delicate white flowers. I kept watering it because the clovers started to yellow and shrivel up. It continued looking like it was drying up, so I gave it fertilizer and more water. Out of desperation, I did what you **should do for all of life's mysteries**—I looked it up on the web. I found pictures of other shamrock plants that looked as sad as mine. The root of the problem was indeed water, but it was either too much or too little. **Shamrocks, and many other plants I've** learned, look equally pitiful when you ignore them as when you give them lots of love and water. **Then there's the shamrock dormancy period, which I can** understand for bulbs that must freeze over in the winter and bears that hibernate during the cold months. But I do not understand dormancy for shamrocks, other than blooming just around St. **Patrick's Day, but that can't be right.**

To diagnose whether it's under or over watering, you're supposed to stick your finger in the dirt and make a proclamation. I stuck my non-green thumb on the top of the soil, which seemed as arid as the Mohave Desert, and so gave my near-death shamrock more water. After lamenting to my work pal René about my unlucky shamrock, she let me in on the clue to successful growing—a moisture meter.

So if you're a gardener tending to house plants or garden plants that don't look in the peak of health, before you pour one more drop of water on anything, go and get yourself a moisture meter. A moisture meter is like a meat thermometer—it has a long pointy spike with an egg-sized indicator opposite the pointy end. Instead of letting you know when your pork is hot enough so it won't poison you, a moisture meter tells you when you're drowning your plant. These meters can get all fancy, but mine has only *dry*, *moist* and *wet* indications.

My plants only get watered when the meter reads *dry*. Only after three weeks of daily readings did my beloved shamrock start reading *dry* and that's when it got a drink. I have to say that my pretty shamrock is now perky and cheerful. I'm glad I no longer depend on a moisture-sensing finger—its retirement was long overdue and the new technology that replaced it works like a lucky charm.

Nothing Close to the Truth

The first time I was called for jury duty, I was dismayed. I had heard stories of how you sit in a room all day, maybe were called for a panel, then you had to answer some questions, then they let you go home. Of course, I had to show up, but my friends all advised that if you didn't want to get selected for an actual jury then, during the Q&A, you should make your answers so obviously one-sided that no one in their right mind would choose you. Otherwise you may have to put your daytime responsibilities on hold for a week or so while you get educated on the whole judicial process and weigh the evidence with a group of strangers who gave fair and impartial responses during the Q&A session.

When I told my boss that I wouldn't be in on Monday since my civic duty called, he just laughed and said that *NO WAY* would they choose me, an engineer, to be on a jury. The best candidates, he claimed, where those who could be swayed by emotions, and engineers are taught to deal with just the facts. This was the guy who earned a PhD in material science and served as an expert witness in many a trial where he presented his lab analysis of objects or materials that failed in the line of duty and caused sufficient bodily or financial harm to warrant a lawsuit. He knew lawyers inside and out and joked that I should tell the jury-picking lawyers that if the person wasn't guilty, they wouldn't be there. I remember hearing something about contempt of court, so I wasn't planning on taking his advice on that point.

So off I went, sat in a room, got called for a panel, and found myself facing *really* young-looking lawyers asking questions about being fair and impartial regarding a young driver who failed a breathalyzer test because he inhaled glue all day during his carpet-installation job and not because of what he drank when he stopped at a bar on the way home. All on the panel were asked a question or two, except for me. I hoped they decided to ignore me, but not so lucky. "Oh, we missed you, ma'am. Do you feel it's possible to have a false reading on a breathalyzer due to other circumstances?" My answer, after every other person had answered "*yes*" was "*no.*"

The child-lawyer froze and looked quite stunned, then asked me to explain. "Well, my husband was part of the team that produced data to certify the breathalyzer test for use by the police. The alcohol in carpet glue is a different composition than the alcohol in drinks, so there's no possibility that inhaling glue would produce a false positive," I calmly said in my best engineer voice. The legal teams asked for a moment, went into a huddle, then dismissed the entire panel and I got to go home.

I told my husband about letting everyone in the room know that breathalyzers can detect the difference between glue and beer—all thanks to him! My husband froze and looked quite stunned. "I never told you that!" What he *did* tell me is that he got drunk a few times during controlled experiments where they measured his blood alcohol level and compared it to the breathalyzer method to ensure it was calibrated correctly. Apparently, my brain made up the rest about the different alcohol types. I asked him if it could *possibly* be true, and his answer was *probably not*.

What my boss said about engineers being lousy jurors may indeed be true. But in my case, it's true because I'm swayed by my overactive imagination rather than emotions.

Lite Bites

Wisdom with Age

"With age comes wisdom." Thank goodness for that because there's a lot of other crap that can invade your wisest years. It's easy to dwell on failing eyesight, failing memories, and failing body parts, but those of us considered to be *mature* earned some features we should be proud of.

Studies show that happiness increases as you move through your golden years. Some are happy that we've lasted so long, while others are happy when we realize it may actually be a choice. If happiness is a choice, then unhappiness is another choice. I know which one I'm picking.

Storytelling is another ability that develops with age. Some stories get repeated lots of times, so you can remember the audience's reaction and refine it so the good parts are emphasized and the not-so-good parts get edited out. Sort of like stand-up comedy—the monologue gets polished with each telling until it flows clearly and smoothly. Some good stories are even told by those who heard them from others rather than actually experiencing it themselves. This has to do with false memories, which also come with age, but fortunately so does increased indifference for little mistakes people make that don't matter so much in the big picture. It all evens out.

And grasping the big picture is a big deal on our journey to wisdom because the small things aren't really important. Experience requires aging, but is very valuable to skillfully navigate life when it throws curve balls. When you're five years old and don't like your birthday cake, it's an end-of-world tragedy.

Lite Bites

When your 55 and your birthday cake turns out crappy, well, so what? The next cake you eat will probably be delicious.

Empathy is another trait that tracks its growth with the more birthdays you celebrate. The more you've experienced, the more you can grasp what someone else is feeling. The reason that's important is that everyone wants to hear they'll get through some challenge successfully because lots of other folks have. The safety-in-numbers thing is big—no one wants to be the only one on the island.

Self-confidence grows with age. Remember that awkwardness of your teens? Do you want ever feel that way again? Enough said.

You make better decisions as you grow older, the experts claim. The experience you gain after making bad decisions gives you that wisdom needed to make better ones. How many times have you said, "Well I won't ever do that again!" It's the voice of experience, sometimes learned by the voice of a parent saying, "You better never do that again!"

People aren't the only things that get better with age. Think about wine, cheese, those favorite jeans and your best friend. All are better now than they were before, thanks to the passage of time. But of all the things that develop with time, it's wisdom I cherish the most, because that's what allows you to cope with the aching backs, creaking knees, and a need for an afternoon nap every so often.

This section started with a quote from Oscar Wilde. Actually, the full quote is, "With age comes wisdom, but sometimes age comes alone." Don't know about you, but I'm refusing to buy into the "alone" part.

Lite Bites

Lite Bites

Look at it This Way

Lite Bites

My Favorite Holiday

Most people say that Christmas is their favorite holiday, but I say that ho-ho Holiday has nothing on **all the good that's stuffed into Thanksgiving. Just** think about it: roasted turkey is delicious and **something you don't eat every day; stressing over buying or receiving presents isn't part of the deal; the day always falls on a** Thursday, making for a four-day weekend; and you can celebrate at home or at your favorite restaurant. Without any religious overtones, there are **no hard feelings over someone's** deity preference.

The ritual is the same, so you can spend the day with family, friends, neighbors, or strangers without being uncomfortable about who does what or what happens next. Football watching is part of the deal, but you can choose to nap to whatever TV station is on or even to your favorite music.

If your bird day is happening at home, just plan on preparing for **hours on end to make the traditional day's fare of turkey, stuffing,** cranberry sauce and various side dishes involving veggies and starches. You must have two choices of pie, one being pumpkin, and make sure to enlist a clean-up crew.

Before stuffing your pie hole, a nice touch is to say out loud what **you're thankful for. If you can't think of anything, you can't go** wrong just mentioning **the people around you or the feast you're** about to dive into.

What I'm thankful for these days is that many fine restaurants offer a scrumptious bird buffet. Back in the day, eating establishments **would be closed, but now it's wise to leave the feast preparation to** professionals. The only shortcoming of this approach is the lack of leftovers. But really, who has room in their refrigerators for all that's left over from a feast for 20 that's prepared for a table of just six? What happens to gravy after a day in the fridge isn't very appetizing.

Some may point out that the 4th of July has a lot of the same advantages; a festive feast, without the presents, the weather is usually more pleasant, with fireworks added in. Although fireworks are really thrilling, the chance of snotty weather or unwelcome crawling, flying, and biting insects can make Independence Day feel less than liberating. Those who watched *How It's Made* on the Discovery Channel may find the fare less tempting knowing what parts of the pig go into a hot dog.

Then there's New Year's. Increasing age has brought me a sincere appreciation for routine sleeping hours, and drinking and driving these days just isn't happening. Speaking of drinking, St. Patrick's Day has a special place in my heart due to my Irish lineage, but there's not much that can be done to improve a boiled dinner of corned beef and cabbage other than another beer. Valentine's Day is sweet, but the celebration is focused on couples, and singles are singled out. Gift inequity can also be awkward. "Wow, these diamond earrings are beautiful! I hope you like the boxer shorts just as much."

So that brings us back to Thanksgiving. It's the one holiday I'm most thankful for.

Lite Bites

Actually, Numbers Do Lie

They say that baseball is the sport with the most **superstitions, and it's obviously true. As I** cheered for my local team in the playoffs, the announcer said the opposing team was supposed to wear white jerseys that night, but some statistician calculated that they won many more games in their red jerseys, so red is what they wore. Since those guys were dressed in red, my home team decided to wear their blue jerseys since they won an overwhelming percentage of games while dressed in blue.

I can just hear the chatter in the locker room. The catcher asks the **shortstop, "Hey dude, does this color make** me look like a **winner?" The shortstop answers, "Why yes, we've won 37% more games in our blue uniforms than our whites."** The focus on trying to score more runs to win the game is out in left field.

The misapplication of numbers continues. A left-handed relief pitcher gets put in the game for one batter who has a 0 of 18 record hitting lefties. For every calculation, there's reality that doesn't pay attention to stats. The leftie proceeded to hit the first pitch out of the park. "We've never seen that before!" the announcers exclaim. But they don't really know that. It was an information feed provided by a group of statisticians who accesses gigabytes of sports minutia in fractions of seconds.

Manipulation of numbers to make a point extends to other sports. On the first day of football season, someone always says, "You can't have an undefeated season if you lose the first game." Football may be guilty of manipulation of the most numbers, which is amazing for a sport with less than 20 games in a season. But a lot of stats are needed to feed endless talk shows, pre-game hype, post-game analysis and, of course, fantasy football.

Lite Bites

The numbers game extends far beyond sports. Politicians believe the polls only when they serve their campaign. Law enforcement uses the decreasing crime rate to demonstrate its ability to keep the peace. But the medical community takes the cake when it comes to manipulating numbers to support whatever conclusion wants to be drawn by those sponsoring the study. We all know that statisticians get paid to torture numbers until they confess.

We were introduced to *4 out of 5 dentists recommend sugarless gum for their patients who chew gum* in the 1970s. No mention was made of whether they interviewed 5 or 5,000 dentists to come to that conclusion, and back then, we were too naïve to ask. Since the 70s, there have been 782,912 conclusions from dentist interviews without one of them being statistically significant. If you don't believe that number, you are among the 93.4% of the population who doesn't believe anything they read. (I could also mention that 84% of the statistics quoted in casual conversation are made up on the spot, but I just made that up.)

But what about the numbers you want to believe? Do you really think that eating dark chocolate every day reduces your chances of heart disease by 34%? Can 10 minutes of exercise a day make you as fit as the model on the TV ad? What about coffee? Scientists have been studying that beverage so much that anything you want to believe has a medically proven basis in some study done somewhere.

Before you go changing what you put in your mouth, it's important to get the details behind the numbers. The fifth dentist actually recommended no gum chewing at all, and Zurich, Switzerland, hardly unbiased, is where the heart health benefits of chocolate were "discovered." But wait, a new report says 87.3% of the Swiss have no interest whatsoever in increasing the chocolate consumption of the world. Now I feel better.

Lite Bites

Mourning the Soap Loss

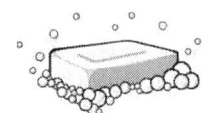

It tickles me to open new packages and I'm not talking just presents. Opening the things brought home in grocery bags is one of life's little thrills to be fully enjoyed. A bag full of coffee beans is my absolute favorite. As soon as I break the air-tight seal, I stick my schnozzola deep into those beans and take a big whiff. Then I take three more.

A new box of cereal is another happy opening event. Seeing all those unbroken flakes that rest on top can start a day off just right. It can make you forget about the cereal dust settled on the bottom that must be dealt with at a later time. Unwrapping a new bar of soap is another favorite. It's not yet sticky or slippery so it's a time to cherish the only stage in the bar's life when it is easy to handle.

Recently, my soap-opening delight was dashed when I found a new bar to be a skinnied-down version of the size I was familiar with since childhood. Apparently, hard economic times forced the manufacturer to downsize the bar by 20%.

I know it's 20% because not long after my discovery, a consumer advocate report did the calculation for me. My lifelong soap fave was featured on TV as one of the many items that's secretly being scrimped on while carrying the same price tag. This down-sizing has affected everything from laundry detergent to orange juice to potato chips. Even toilet paper is wasting away. For years, that cardboard tube inside a TP roll could be cleverly repurposed to serve as a band to keep unruly extension cords neatly coiled. These days, that band is about an inch narrower. We're getting fewer inches and ounces for our money, and it's just not right. But it's even more not right when applied to bar soap.

There comes a time in a bar's life when it just becomes too thin to be useful. You can try to stick it to a new bar, but soap fusion is as elusive as atomic fusion. By starting out with 20% less soap, the stage at which soap becomes aggravatingly small is reached much sooner.

It's not unlike peaches and pomegranates. The pits in peaches take up a small fraction of the fruit, so you can get enough peach in you before the need to deal with the pit. On the other hand, eating a pomegranate is best left to those with saintly patience. The eatable portion of a pomegranate versus the seed is so lopsided that it's hardly worth the effort.

So let's gets back to soap. An option I considered is to use the liquid soap that comes in a big bottle, but it's just not the same. A dollop of the liquid soap doesn't offer as many bubbles and clean as much body real estate as what you get from a few scrapes across a washcloth from a bar. It's a density thing: solids are just more concentrated than goopy liquids. Also, my shower stall is equipped with a place for a bar of soap. Another bottle would just vie for the space on the rack that's used for shampoo and conditioner, and I don't need any more options that may cause confusion in the morning.

With smaller soap bars, the fraction of usable soap is actually much less than the 20% of weight reduction since the unusable portion doesn't change. Therefore, the frequency with which new soap must be bought is more than 20%. It's a vicious downward spiral that I'm sure the soap manufacturers didn't think about. If they did, they would have done the honorable thing and just increased the price.

It's Time!

My alarm clock was set at 5 a.m. for decades because it took an hour to become presentable and another hour to get to work by 7 a.m. My beloved also got up at 5 a.m. because he liked getting up early, wanted to read the paper, check his email and hang for a while before his tee time. People who knew our morning routine don't understand any of it. I don't golf. He doesn't work. We're in bed by 10:30 p.m. With this routine, it's hard to get in sync with the rest of the world on the weekends, even if we sleep in until 6 a.m.

For example, it's 8 a.m. on Sunday morning. "Let's call Wayne and Karol to see if they want to go to lunch," he says. "Let's wait until we know they're up," I say. "They have to be up," he says pointing to the watch he's been watching for two hours. We left a message, and the call was returned at 10 a.m. They haven't eaten breakfast yet, so a lunch discussion is not on the menu.

Fast forward to today; I'm retired from working full-time work, so I work my own hours—yeah! These days, the gentle wake-up melody on the cell phone plays at 5:30 a.m. Not a big difference, but I'll take every minute I can get. When you rise at that hour and eat breakfast, you're setting the dining timing for the rest of the day. Stomach growls start around 11:30, and they must be tamed. That means dinner by 6 p.m. or maybe earlier. When smaller, more mature appetites join the necessity for digestion before lying down, early-bird deals are something to flock to.

During evening hours, reading, TVing, jigsaw puzzling, emailing, writing or pre-sleep napping take up time. There's a time for everything, and everything in due time, they say. There are 24 hours in a day, but on some days, time seems to drag on. Other days, time flies. Time heals all wounds. Everyone wants more time, because many times, we're out of time. Time waits for no one.

It's good to be on time, and that's really hard to explain to a toddler. "It's time to go," I say to grandchild from the running car with door open waiting for his entry, and I'm realizing we're going to be late. Said child is mesmerized by a bug crawling on a leaf and will not budge. "I'm not hungry." But it's dinner time. They're never sleepy when it's bedtime. The world's on a timetable, and kids are having nothing to do with it.

During your career, you need to arrive to work on time, come to meetings on time, and more importantly, wrap up meetings when time's up. A colleague chattering away about something you couldn't care less about is wasting your time, and that likely means you'll be working overtime.

My first real job was at IBM, and its museum showed the origin of the company as International Time Recording. In the 1920s and 1930s, the company made punch clocks. Punching in and punching out of work on time was very important during those times. Those antique clocks sell for about $600 on eBay, and that just proves that time is money.

Can't Find the Words

Emojis are taking over our written language, and I'm filing a formal complaint. Long, long ago, before there were letters and language and Number 2 pencils, people carved pictures on cave walls to describe how the tribe hunted or the recipe for cooking a large beast. Since then, our intelligent species evolved and developed an alphabet and words and the printing press. Fast forward to present day: we've reverted back to using pictures to communicate. And I'm just not OK with all this. I love words. I love clever phrases. I love rhyming words. I love all that's alliteration and I love finding the origins of odd sayings. And I'm not pulling your leg.

Now I ask you: Does anyone love emojis other than the original yellow smiley face? You can't read a text full of emojis out loud. My car tries when I get a text while driving, but Bluetooth becomes Blue-tongue-tied when the inputs are images. Maybe it's because emojis' purpose is to convey a sentiment, and sentiments can't be articulated. Maybe that explains why there's no emoji for *word*. Maybe that's three more reasons why I lodged a complaint against emojis. We should know how to convey sentiments using actual words.

There are over 3,000 emojis. To learn that many words it takes a person the first five years of life. I'll guess it takes a texter about 5 minutes to learn 3,000 emojis. But I just don't get a lot of them. The faces *should* be easy, but what emotion is captured by shifted eyes and a mouth shifted in the same direction? And what about the crying eyes but laughing mouth? I've read that this is the most misunderstood emoji around. Since emojis are to make conveying messages easier, the crying/laughing face just isn't up to par.

Not only are emojis invading texts, they're now migrating to the subject line of spam. Very clever to add a little icon in there to get people to open spam! I'm ashamed to admit that it worked on me. Then I had to figure out how to send an email with a little picture in the subject line. That took some time. Hint: just type it into the body of the email, then cut and paste it into the subject line.

And what about the tons of emojis that just look like things: flowers, animals, salt shakers? One would think it would be easier to type in the word rather than look through a mountain of emojis to find what you're thinking of. You won't be surprised that there is a translator on the web to go from words to emojis and back, sort of like what *Google Translate* does with languages that people actually speak, with their mouths.

Now that my complaint is filed, it's time for an admission: I use emojis. But they are reserved for appropriate emphasis after all words required to convey the message are typed. There are hearts for my sweetheart, hugs for my friends, thumbs up to show appreciation for co-workers and food emojis when texting dinner plans. That's it. ☺

My Favorite Hobby

If someone asked me what my favorite hobby is, I would honestly answer cleaning house—even though it is a very stupid answer on so many levels. But think about it: a hobby gives you satisfaction, you can enjoy the results when you're done, you can compare techniques with friends, you spend some time at it every week, you need special tools that get upgraded when something new is on the market, it burns calories, you can do too much and go overboard—I can go on forever, but I think you get my drift.

My two Barb friends are in the elite category of cleaning hobbyists. One just told me that it felt so good to take EVERYTHING out of EVERY kitchen cabinet, and wash all the dishes, pots, pans, utensils, bake pans, cups, glasses, and serving trays in the dishwasher. She wiped down the inside and outside of the cabinets before returning the cleaned items to their rightful spots. That's a bit much for me; I only do that when I buy a new house. But this is the gal who can spot insect pee on her windows. My other Barb friend once told me she dusted her walls. I can understand dusting the baseboards, but never knew wall dusting was a thing. Just like with sports, the appropriate way to react to such high levels of performance is not to be ashamed of your own shortcomings, but to learn from the masters and give them praise for rising to such a level of proficiency.

When I ran some gizmo over to my neighbor's house the other day, I remarked how nice her house smelled. Her 45-minute rather-interesting response involved the new-found cleaner she was using on the acres of tile that were in her house, her current method of cleaning (which I want to try) and the last four unsatisfactory methods of cleaning (two of which I currently use.)

She opined having her tile buffed, so now she has me thinking about that. I asked her how to clean the grout without resorting to getting on your hands and knees with a toothbrush. She didn't know, but she'll find out and get back to me. There we were, two educated individuals, comparing miniscule details and the pros and cons of steam cleaning versus the spinning mop thingy that comes with a big bucket that's too heavy to lug around the house.

Of course, house cleaning as a hobby isn't for everyone. A few of our friends pay for a service to make their home sparkle. One couple remarked how their cleaning person got rid of all the grease, dirt, and gritty grime to turn their sticking doors back into sliding doors. The glass on said doors was buffed to a shine so that no fingerprint would dare to linger. While they get satisfaction for choosing the right cleaning service, I get satisfaction from doing the service myself.

And isn't that what hobbies are all about? You spend time doing something that brings you joy, sometimes while doing it, but mostly when you can enjoy the results. But that's enough about cleaning for now; it's time to go vacuum the back porch.

On a Roll

Of all the things that come on rolls, aluminum foil and wax paper are my favorite in the kitchen. The starting end is always at hand, it's easy to pull off the length you need, tear it cleanly and then put it away. If you need to roll up some excess after the tear, it's easy-peasy. No sweat!

To the contrary, plastic wrap is a whole different kettle of fish, as some say in some kitchens somewhere. It can take forever to find the end, which is actually the start. When you pull it, you sometimes begin tearing off a small ribbon of wrap rather than the whole roll width. And when you're lucky enough to get to the right width and right length, the whole tearing off process can be tearfully frustrating.

On my kitchen-roll list, paper towels are near the bottom, a smidgen above plastic wrap. Excessive glue holding the first square causes it to shred into unusable pieces and it sometimes brings along a few other sheets. Once started, the roll gets mounted on the paper-towel flagpole. From there, two hands are needed to tear off the sheets to prevent too-many sheets from unrolling or shredding sheets into streamers. Let me ask you: How often do you have two free hands when you urgently need a paper towel? The correct answer is *never*.

But getting back to plastic wrap, an interesting tidbit is that the Saran Wrap name came from the inventor who was a girl dad to Sara and Ann. I'm sure they were fine young girls, but it's clear to me that clear wrap may be too much for the average kitchen worker to grapple with. So let's investigate alternatives.

Lite Bites

<u>Plastic containers</u>. I'm sure mother earth is gasping a bit at these things going into landfills. For me, the plastic doesn't cut it when rewarming leftovers in the microwave. It took me a long time to toss my favorite container after tomato sauce was overheated in it. The milky colored plastic turned pink and the level at the top of the sauce was marked by a ring of blisters.

<u>Plastic bonnets.</u> I found these in the supermarket at a checkout line where your defenses are down and you'll put anything in your cart if you think it will ease kitchen chores. Trust me when I say there's a reason why you probably never heard of these little shower caps for bowls.

<u>Rubbery toppers.</u> Now these are cool. They're made of some special rubbery stuff, are colorfully designed to look like flowers or lily pads or other flat things found in nature, and they simply get slapped on top of your bowl. Like many cool things, they are found at flea markets. Each has a little grab point in the center like a knob on a pot lid. When they are situated right, you can lift your bowl of leftovers by that grab point since the rubbery stuff has made an air-tight seal with the rim of your bowl. The drawback is that they have Goldilocks syndrome—some are too big, some are too small, and unless you have a really big collection, it's hard to get one that fit's just right to the rim of your bowl.

So now we're back to the hunt for the end of the plastic wrap. I don't have a solution to this dilemma, so I'll just wish you happy hunting!

Lite Bites

Shower Power

I love to start my days with a strong, steamy cup of coffee and a strong, steamy shower, but naturally, not at the same time. Because many people are shower-stall dawdlers I can understand the premise behind low-flow shower heads to conserve water. But not me. There's no lingering during the wet phase, but I do take my time during the toweling-off phase, and, since it doesn't use any natural resources, I leisurely intersperse toweling off with the shower-squeegee phase. So, while my shower-water pressure is likely well over the prescribed limit because I had my plumber adjust some gizmos installed by the builder, my time with water flowing is proportionally less. It all balances out, right?

Whenever my morning ritual happens away from home, there's some trepidation about the operation and performance of an unknown shower. My sweetie is the first to rise and check out the shower specifications. When he emerges squeaky clean, he gets the barrage of questions. How fast does the water flow? How long does it take to get hot? How easy is it to adjust the temperature? Are there any tricks with the faucets? Is the soap any good? Do we need to use the conditioner we brought from home? If the first answer indicates the flow is similar to a soft, summer rain, I have to brace myself for a long, arduous process of rinsing off shampoo and soap. But if the answer includes the words *power washer*, I'm in for a treat.

Unfortunately, a hotel shower can have other drawbacks beside a slow drizzle. Stepping into a tub to take a shower is just plain wrong. I don't know why someone doesn't have the nerve to admit that shower curtains don't really work. And if you're not dealing with a shower curtain, you have that way-too-close shower door that gets elbow bumped a few times during cleansing. And having

- 82 -

your whole arm get a cold-water shot when you first turn on a misplaced faucet is just inexcusable.

In spite of the less-than-OK showers I've taken in hotels, usually all offer tiny little bottles of good-smelling shampoo and conditioner. Sometimes, they even match the theme of the little soaps. Exotic Coral. Essence of Bermuda. Minnie Mouse. All have pleasing scents that can compensate for other bathroom shortcomings. I noticed that in the breakfast cafeteria at "The Happiest Place on Earth," I and those around me who were freshly showered smelled like Minnie Mouse soap. It was a nice start to a magical day.

All in all, I've had truly pleasurable shower accommodations while traveling. During my first trip to Mexico, I was introduced to an enormous room with beautiful hand-painted tiles and a shower head near a corner. There was a drain in the floor close by. The sink and loo were in the same room, but far away from the shower head. It was a shower arena without stall walls and it was glorious.

I was introduced to a similar but different concept in Las Vegas when Caesars Palace ran out of regular rooms for trade-show attendees, of which I was one. They were in a pinch, so I was given a love nest. Mirrors on the ceiling I don't need, but there was a wall-free showering area in the middle of the bedroom. What happened in Vegas…was a very good trade show.

Lite Bites

Buon Appetito

I don't remember special recipes from my Irish upbringing, but I do remember wonderful Italian food that my best friend's mom would share since Italians prepare enough for six times the number of guests they're expecting. I haven't found anyone who doesn't like Italian food, and that's because it's basically comfort with cheese. Ask four people what their favorite Italian dish is, and you'll probably get six answers. And they'll be using their hands when they tell you, likely pressing the tips of their first and middle fingers to their thumb.

Typically, when a group agrees they're going for Italian, it's pasta with sauce and pizza. There are so many names for pasta because each time it was shaped a little differently it was given its own label. Starting with angel hair (skinny spaghetti) through to ziti (long tubes), some say there are more than 300 different types of pasta. I say all are good, even though I haven't had more than a dozen.

In Italy, where eating is an exalted experience above all others except for religious ones, there are something like eight courses for dinner. Admittedly, two of these courses are alcoholic drinks, but still, that's a lot of eating going on. That may be why Italian restaurants featuring pasta and pizza serve such large portions—they're paying homage to the homeland, so the salad-and-entrée-two-course dinner gets outsized and served on one gigantic plate. "That's so much food!" is a thinly veiled complaint from someone planning to take home enough for three more dinners.

At our favorite upscale Italian restaurant, owner Luigi greets you at the door, gives the men a bear hug, graciously bends to kiss the ladies' hands and walks you to your table while weaving a story of how hard the chef worked all day blending fresh ingredients with aged cheeses to make the specials. Luigi is the size of a linebacker and talks about food with the passion of a new lover. It is a memorable experience, and all this occurs before snap-unfolding the napkins he places on your lap and passing out five-pound menus.

The other end of the Italian restaurant spectrum is straightforward pizza. **Everyone's favorite type of pizza is a little different, and** probably based on what they ate growing up. In my hometown, there was Vince the Pizza Prince. His orange cheese was sprinkled with a secret blend of spices to create a pie like I have never seen or tasted anywhere else. The glands in the back of my throat ache just thinking about it because it was absolutely the best pizza in the world. And this is the same proclamation made by everyone else about their hometown pizza version.

The Italians save the best for last, and tiramisu is arguably the best dessert in the world. Who else would think to blend rum-soaked lady fingers with mascarpone cheese except chefs who know that the only thing better than a lot of cheese is more cheese?

Some folks know they're Italian by genealogy. I believe I'm Italian by gastronomy.

One Ripe Banana

"At her age, I would only buy one ripe banana a day," our sage friend Jim said on more than one occasion. He may have picked this up from comedian George Burns who, when asked how old he was, quipped, "Well, I don't buy green bananas." You get their meaning—when you're up in years, you really can't count on being around much longer or even hungry for banana tomorrow. Nonetheless, every weekly trip to the grocery store, I grab a bunch of bananas. Other fruit needs to be squeezed, smelled, priced and seasonally evaluated before purchase, but no nonsense like that for bananas. There's something special about bananas, and I don't think they get their due respect for such an apeeling fruit.

I read somewhere that Bananas are the World's Most Perfect Food. It's easy to get to the fruit part, not like oranges or grapefruit that need utensils and some craftiness. One serving size is one banana. Too easy. Cantaloupes and watermelon require big knives, paper towels for juice clean up and plastic wrap to store what's left over. Cherries and berries need to bunch up to get enough for one serving. Based on my grocery store trips, bananas are plentiful and have cost about 69-cents a pound since forever. Banana season is 12 months a year.

Nutritionists say bananas have fiber, antioxidants and nutrients that are hard to come by, all for about 100 calories. They claim to moderate blood-sugar levels and are digestion friendly. Your heart pumps better because of the potassium packaged in this produce. Bananas are kind to your kidneys, and some folks believe they lessen leg cramping. All this makes it the *top banana* in the fruit world.

"What about the apple?" you may say. An apple a day keeps the you-know-who away. Well, dietitians say the banana wins, hands down. Besides, I don't know about you, but the variability in apples ranging from wonderfully crisp and juicy to dry and pithy, makes the humble banana a winner for consistency. If you want variety, pick another fruit. There's pretty much one type of banana. There are plantains, but they're not really bananas, are they?

Bananas have even smooshed their way into music. Remember Harry Chapin's song *30,000 Pounds of Bananas* about a truck driver that lost control during a delivery to Scranton? Decades before this, Louis Prima sang *Yes, We Have No Bananas*. Apparently, banana songs are more about loss than enjoyment.

Bananas ripen in a few days. If bananas survive until old age, they can become delicious bread or muffins. But the best banana buddy may be ice cream. Even though ice-cream plays the starring role, the dessert is called a banana split. When it grew up, it became Bananas Foster and included butter, brown sugar, cinnamon, dark rum, banana liqueur and fire. Order one of these before you die, please.

Our vocabulary is filled with bananas. Someone super excited is *going bananas*. Someone who's that way all the time may be *one banana short of a bunch*. The woman who should not buy green bananas has *one foot in the grave and the other on a banana peel*.

According to experts on such things, the easier way to peel a banana is the other way. What we call the top of the banana is actually the stem. The other end is really the top, and you should always peel a banana from the top. This has been verified in my kitchen and by primates all over the world so I consider it a fact.

Lite Bites

What about the article that claims the *World's Most Perfect Food* is a banana? It was written by, you guessed it, Chiquita. While this may cause you to squint, call me a believer.

Lite Bites

All Work

Lite Bites

Stringy Email

If you haven't noticed, email has become today's version of the chain letter, which actually has its origins during biblical times. I know that's true because I read it on the web. Someone has a thought, writes it down, sends it to someone who adds their own thoughts and sends it on to someone else, and on it goes.

When this was done back in the '70s, postage stamps were used and the process would go on for weeks or months, and perhaps some creative or novel thought did get added along the chain. Back then, the recipients were threatened that if they broke the chain some bad luck, poor health, financial woes, or other misfortune would befall them, so there was incentive to send the letter on to one's friends and relatives who would also get wrapped up in preserving their welfare.

Today, only a small percentage of spam mail carries threats if they are not forwarded, and we all know how to hit the *Delete* key. However, the majority of regular old emails have a magic spell that prevents the recipient from just reading it, hitting *Delete* and moving on with their lives.

Many of today's email strings require a dozen or more presses of the *Pg Dn* key to see what the original thought was. More often than not, the topic in the most current email is far removed from the original person's intention to inform or get informed. But the subject line *never* gets changed. So, reading an email with the subject *Tuesday's Meeting Agenda* can lead you down a path of who's on vacation, what topic was covered in an unrelated meeting, meeting rooms being refurbished, conflicting appointments, and, of course, questions about who's bringing the bagels for a meeting that may or may not have been held on some Tuesday in the distant past.

What makes these emails so maddening is the repetitive use of the "Reply All" key. If you're unfortunate enough to be on the original email distribution, you can have dozens or more emails with the same subject in a matter of hours—maybe minutes if it's a slow day.

A good example of this is a co-worker sending out a photo of his or her newborn baby to a lengthy distribution list. Some folks are getting the email because they actually want to see another photo of a newborn baby. Others are getting it as a reminder of why the new parent won't be in work for a while or will be suffering from sleep deprivation. But why is it that the majority of recipients of said email will hit *Reply All* with a message of congratulations, comments on what a beautiful baby or some other typical response? Even if I did want to see another newborn photo, I certainly didn't want to see 23 responses that cannot possibly say anything that hasn't already been said about a newborn. But I have to read them all since someone will slip in a notice about a meeting I'm supposed to be at on Tuesday where they're having bagels, which I love.

Perhaps we should adopt a modification to a message found at the bottom of some emails: *Think before you print this email—B Green.* My version would read: *Think before you hit "Reply All" to this email—B Sane.*

She Can Act, Too

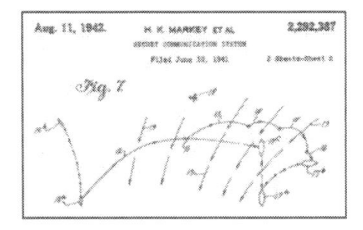

It grabs your attention when someone makes a huge impact in a field that's far afield from their chosen profession. Most of us mortals work hard just to get through the workday. But there is a select minority whose endeavors truly advance the state of their craft and actually advance the human experience. They're the ones that get accolades, medals, fancy titles, wings of buildings named for them and catered retirement parties if they ever decide to leave work, which they don't.

Yet a more austere category exists for those leaders with superpowers not only in their well-known field, but they play in multiple fields. They're called polymaths. We learn about some of these geniuses in school. Ben Franklin was a politician who invented the lightning rod. These are supposed to be two separate skill sets, unlike today's politicians who become lightning rods to divert energy away from more important topics. Leonardo da Vinci was known for his art, but we've all seen his drawings of inventions and detailed sketches of the anatomy, which make him an inventor and an anatomist in addition to a darn good Mona Lisa painter.

Our friend Marti's undergraduate degree is in music, and it was obtained after a full concert recital. She then earned her law degree and was a very successful practicing lawyer. Then she started a winery with her husband, and the wines they crafted earned lots of medals. There's no doubt she's brilliant, but if her multiple ventures were a Venn diagram, there would scarcely be overlap. The only logical explanation is that she has three brains.

Lite Bites

And then there's colleague Randy, a genius, gray-beard engineer whom other engineers gravitate to for guidance and wisdom on work and career problems. In his spare time, Randy is a woodworker. Photos of his art, which also serve as useful items like a jewelry box, are amazing. But what is most amazing about Randy is his photography. He doesn't just snap a few pics of an interesting view. Randy travels far and wide around the planet, often during typical non-waking hours and/or adverse weather conditions, to position himself at a place with a *really interesting* view and he shoots away. He then spends hours retouching pixels to remove lens flare and tiny imperfections imperceptible to anyone else on earth. In my opinion, Ansel Adams had nothing on Randy but name recognition and a pro marketing machine.

How about Austrian-born Hedwig Markey, who was inducted into the National Inventors Hall of Fame for her torpedo guidance system that used frequency-hopping spread-spectrum technology? Figure 7 from her patent is at the start of this story. You may be picturing Hedwig as a plain-looking, solitary bookworm, but not so fast. While dating Howard Hughes, she also contributed ideas to improve aircraft aerodynamics. She was also a movie producer, which may explain why she traveled in the same circles as Hughes, known for spending time with beautiful women. Indeed, she was promoted as "the world's most beautiful woman" by the head of MGM studios, Louis B. Mayer, who also called this scientist by her stage name—Hedy Lamarr. Yep, *that* Hedy Lamarr, producer and film star of yesteryear who figured out anti-jamming techniques that served as the basis for the Bluetooth and Wi-Fi we use today. I am very sure that among the aeronautical engineers I have worked with, the only overlap with the acting profession is that some can recite dialogue from an entire movie scene. Engineers do this because they spent half of their youth watching movies, and it compensates for their inability to make small talk.

Lite Bites

Alternate Reality

What if you learned there was an alternate reality? The language spoken there was only understood by those within. People spent many hours here, but time did not pass in a normal manner; it either sped by or dragged on. The manner of dress was not typical of what was worn outside of this special place. People did not act as they would at home, at a restaurant, with friends, or any other place outside of this reality. Those in this reality were forced to act in accordance with the rules posted throughout or they get banished. Approximately 25% of the people are considered leaders, and their commands are to be obeyed by anyone they chose to command. These leaders read books and study psychology so that they are given more people to command. I'm sure the last clue made you realize this alternate reality is actually the business office of today.

Now many people love their jobs and enjoy working in an office environment. But I'll bet there are more who could rattle off a list of things they would change if given the opportunity. And the infrequent company-sponsored social get-togethers typically feel like work. It is very possible you have nothing in common with coworkers other than, well, work. If there are zero non-work things to discuss with someone, there's less than zero to talk about with their better half. So, when fellow workers babble on with acronym-filled language, the spouses wish it were time to go home soon after arriving.

Maybe this just applies to engineering-type offices, because our type isn't known for easy social interaction and we may use more acronyms than any other career. As the saying goes, you can always spot the extroverted engineer because they're staring at *your* shoes instead of their own. But I'll bet even lawyer spouses would rather be anywhere than chatting up the top legal beagle at the bar while feigning interest the latest court case.

Each year, when our new crop of college interns showed up at the office, I'd advise them, "You are now in an artificial environment created for the sole purpose of the company to make money." They don't understand at first, but in time, they do. "What happens at all-hands meetings?" they ask. "You believe you learn what EBITA[2] means and are shown bar graphs or pie charts that no one really understands," is the answer. "Why can't I work on the cool project?" "Because the cool one isn't funded, and we're behind schedule on the other ones." "Can I take next week off?" "Sure, but do you want to be known as the intern who asked for time off before lunch on your first day of work?"

Finding out what your co-workers do on their time away from the office can be interesting or alarming. Typically, it's the alarming stuff that's discussed way too early and too long on Monday mornings. It's clear that in this artificial environment, you don't choose the people you'll be spending almost half of your waking hours with. They get chosen based on their skills, and a hunch that they'll fit in with the culture, but some just don't.

I've been fortunate to work with many engineers I hold in high regard who have made my office experience a pleasure. I've been lucky to have some engineers chose to leave their old jobs to join the office where I worked. I've been luckier still when I was asked to join an office where others worked. But what I really enjoyed was conversing with my colleagues in our acronym-filled secret language, but *in the office*.

---

[2] In case you are curious, that's "Earnings Before Interest, Taxes, Depreciation, and Amortization".

Lite Bites

The Interview

If you ever held a job, you've gone through an interview. Once you come out the other end of an interview, you'll never be the same. An interview is an artificial creation of the business world surprisingly similar to reading a script to land a role in a movie. The interviewer cues with canned questions, then the candidate recites answers found on the internet. All those involved pretend the interviewer is getting to know the candidate to assess whether they have the right credentials and will fit in the company culture. Unfortunately, no one can assess that accurately within the confines of a 60-minute discussion of pat questions and lies disguised as responses. It may be more cost effective and just as accurate to give each candidate some dice and hire the one who rolls the highest number.

Long ago, job seekers would write a clear, spell-checked résumé, make a bunch of neatly printed copies on nice paper and distribute them to companies like dandelion seeds blowing in the wind. Humans would read the résumés, set up an interview and ask the typical questions. But the world became a bigger place. Now résumés are customized to the job under consideration and then scanned by the placement agency to ensure key words are present. A period of time follows while they are being ignored until the persistent job seeker finds someone who works at the target company and can put in a good word.

Creative-type companies twisted the interview process around. "How many paperclips will reach from the earth to the moon?" Of course the answer doesn't come in the form of a number, but rather a story that gives insight into how clever the candidate is when faced with unanswerable questions—the kind you see every day at work. Nowadays it's fashionable to create a short video to send the company so it can determine the winner of the Oscar for best director from the candidates.

I honestly don't remember any answers I gave while being interviewed, but I do remember some actual responses I've heard as the interviewer:

Question: "Why do you want this position?"
Answer: "Because I like the title."

Question to a young interviewee: "What do you see yourself doing five years from now?"
Answer: "I expect to be in management at a different company."

Question: "If you were hired for this position, what is the first thing you would do?"
Answer: "I'd make everyone clean up the area; this place looks like a dump."

Question: "Why do you want to work for this company?"
Answer: "Well, I was hoping you'd tell me what you do here so I can decide if I want to work here."

The sad part of these real-world examples is that every person giving these answers was offered a job. So not only are interviews a waste of time, the data being collected during them is tossed away. This gets me back to my point of proposing a roll of the dice as the best way for hiring managers to choose the best candidate. But this should be done only after the key-word scanner approves their résumé.

Lite Bites

Office Health

Just like the number of white blood cells indicates the level of invading germs you're fighting, the number of Dilbert comics adorning office walls is an indicator of the level of dumb policies workers are battling. Dilbert's creator, Scott Adams, admits that his readers supply him with endless fodder for his comic strip that way-too-many folks who work in a cube all day can very easily relate to.

Regarding real health, what about those employees who turn a blind eye to everyone else's health and show up for work hacking and coughing up a lung? It took a pandemic to stop that nonsense, but prior to that, it took many co-workers using their loud, outside voices to tell "patient zero" to go straight home.

Some who write books and lecture for a living say office health is measured by the level of cleanliness in the office environs. Those followers of Japanese office productivity methods say everyone should work in an orderly, uncluttered space. While this may be fine for some, the creative engineers I spent decades working with were better aligned with Oscar Madison of the Odd Couple. "A clean stall is the sign of a dead horse" was the sign on Dale's desk, although it was barely visible among all the stacks of books and papers.

Office parents frequently have pictures of their kids on their desk. Everyone knows the ages of the kids in the photos does not represent the ages of the kids in modern times. When I commented on a photo of a young boy missing a front tooth, the dad tells me that kid has one of his own kids in college and another in high school. Speaking of photos, you'd be wise not to comment on the spouse ones. A glamourous pic of one gorgeous woman prompted a co-worker's comment, "Wow, I met her, and she doesn't look anything like that in real life!"

The circle of life, in office-health terms, is on full display after a layoff or resignation. Surviving workers gather around the recently departed's desk to see what furniture or supplies they can scavenge to upgrade what's currently at their own desks. It should surprise no one that the newest member of any department has the chair with the stained seat and the smallest computer display.

And as long as there are people working in offices, there will be office pranks. My favorite was encasing Jim's computer mouse in a quart of yellow Jell-O in honor of his 50th birthday. To be fair, I used a broken mouse that the IT department gave me, but Jim didn't know that when he poked the jiggling mouse mold and wondered how to excavate it.

Not everything that happens in an office is dull and boring. Just look at today's Dilbert cartoon and you're sure to crack a smile and wonder how Scott Adams can possibly know exactly what goes on at your company.

Truth, Straight Up

"You have a booger on your nose." Not many people would say that to a co-worker, but if you did (have a booger on your nose) wouldn't you want to know? In the spirit of truth hurts, but lies hurt more, I tell people when they have stuff that doesn't belong on their face, or their shirt, or their pants, or wherever they're not looking or can't see. They should know about items so they can fix it immediately and limit possible embarrassment. What no one wants to hear is "How long were you going to wait before you told me?" after an hour meeting with that person and five others.

"The elbows on that shirt are worn through," I said to one of my Einstein-brilliant colleagues dressed in a shirt that looked like he pulled it out of a garbage bin. "Oh this is the one! I knew one of my shirts had holes, but I couldn't remember which one," was the casual reply as he rolled up his sleeves to hide the threadbare sections, fortunately also hiding a cigarette burn on one cuff. He thanked me sincerely.

Some folks try to offer help more gently via mimicking, but it's much less efficient. "Go like this," Bruce said as he rubbed his face in front of someone who had a pencil mark on their cheek. "Why should I?" was the response. "Well, there's something there," Bruce mumbled. "What is it?" said the person, who really was more interested in an ID than clearing it up. "Why don't you just go to the men's room to see for yourself?" was the final retort.

There are always buttons needing to be buttoned, flies needing to be zipped (a popular one), and comforter stuffing on your back—all things that should be brought up quickly and clearly to allow for corrections. But then there's another category—wardrobe errors that can't be fixed without changing to something that's usually at home. What about two different shoes (not popular, but memorable) or mismatched socks? I've personally experienced the shoe faux pas when I wore one navy and one black pump of the same style. These not-easy-to-fix gaffes should also be pointed out so the person can then admit the error at the beginning of a gathering to offer an alibi. "I didn't turn the light on in my closet to make sure I had a matched pair, so I guess I'll start a fashion trend," was my story on mixed-pump day.

It was my first meeting in the morning when Jim arrived early and squawked, "What happened? You have mascara all over your face." I think I was more startled that Jim knew what mascara was, but then I remembered pulling a shirt over my head right after applying a few coats of water-proof mascara, which turns into tar after it dries. Since people started to file in for the meeting, I watched Jim as he pointed to areas on his face while I tried to rub clean the same areas on my face. (Note: the successful mimicking technique requires that you present the action as though the subject were looking into a mirror). After he realized it wasn't working, he retreated by saying, "It's really not that bad, but you should check it out when we're done here." I thanked him sincerely, just like he did when I told him he had a booger on his nose.

The Loud One

Every business has at least one, and unfortunately sometimes there are more than one. We all know them—they're the loudest person in the office who thinks everyone wants to, and needs to, hear every word they roar. When they're on the phone, while they're reading an email out loud, when they're typing while dictating to themselves. There is no inside voice with these types. Everything in their head is absolutely incredible, and all their thoughts must be given an outside voice—loud enough so that anyone in the office arena can hear them.

It is not an uncommon to hear "Oh no, here we go again," from *The Loud One* at 90 decibels—something like a gunshot at the start of a race. Only this race is no more than dramatic blabbering about an ordinary incident they think is extraordinary since it happened to them. The only thing worse than listening to *The Loud One* talking to no one in particular is when they're using the speaker phone so you hear both sides of the conversation. Even if the person on the other end is a normal talker, *The Loud One* turns up the volume so you have two louds, and that don't make it right. *The Loud One* thinks that surely everyone wants to hear the entire conversation, so the broadcast continues. Except that no one wants to hear it, because it's not interesting and they're trying to do their own work.

Experts who study human behavior for a living offer many explanations for loud talkers. Perhaps that's the way they were raised. Maybe they are shy and are unknowingly overcompensating. It's possible they could be hard of hearing. The muscles in their throat are over developed. But co-workers who are victims of this aggravating behavior usually see just one reason—*The Loud One* is obnoxious, has no respect for other people's personal space and wants to project themselves as the most important one in the room. I can't say who's right, experts or co-workers, but I can tell you the co-workers surely know *The Loud One* much better having listened to loud chatter many hours a day.

If you're a victim to *The Loud One*, what to do? Going back to the experts, they suggest being patient, understanding and respectful. While that may be appropriate for a stranger during a bus trip, co-workers handle this behavior a little differently. I've seen office doors slammed, telling *The Loud One* to shut up in an even louder voice, and punching the hang-up button on the speaker phone. (I thought it was the mute button, honest!) Unfortunately, none of these solutions work because *The Loud One* needs first to admit there's a problem. And that's the problem, the admission just won't happen.

One way to deal with those without volume control is to put on the noise-cancelling headphones or pop in ear buds and turn up the volume on your music. Or maybe make a phone call and tune the speaker volume up to the max while the on-hold music is playing, but that's sliding down to their level. Maybe the best solution is to overload management with way too many praises of *The Loud One's* performance so they get promoted to another location.

Those Entitled

Long ago, when people had careers and not just jobs, it was customary to share business cards. When you met new people, you'd hand them a card and they'd do the same in return. Cards were stored alphabetically in a Rolodex for future use. The Japanese, who hold traditions dear, still present business cards, and with much ceremony.

While bowing, the card is presented with two hands so the text is properly facing the recipient. The recipient, while bowing, carefully accepts it with the same number of hands and with the care and attention normally used when transferring a new baby or a full-to-the-brim martini. The card is carefully read, than an appropriate small-talk comment is made about some of the information so it demonstrates comprehension and thought. The Japanese are steeped in respect, so you can't not admire them.

Information on your business card includes your name, natch', the company you work for, its logo, phone number, and that all-important identification—your job title. The job title is a sacred part of who you are—in the office anyway. Back in the day, large companies such as IBM had very specific and very telling job titles. Starting at *Junior Worker*, you'd move through *Staff Worker*, then *Senior Staff Worker*, to *Advisory Worker*, *Senior Worker* and maybe on to *Distinguished Worker*. If you were really a smart, high-contributing, well-connected, patent-holding, well-educated worker, the CEO would give you the title of *IBM Fellow*. I was surprised to see that term is still used today, even though many who reached the austere position are *Fellas*, or whatever the female version of fellow is.

I was once introduced to a sage scientist who had the business-card title *Quantum Mechanics Philosopher*. I didn't understand his explanation of that role, but I did understand his explanation of how that title landed on his card. He went to the company's on-line card-ordering system and found they not only eliminated the drop-down menu that limited title choices to those sanctioned by the company, there was no limit on the number of characters you could type in. Hence, *Quantum Mechanics Philosopher* was what he felt best suited his role at the company, and besides, it was cool. I have no memory of what the meeting was about, but I'll always remember that dude and our chance, one-time encounter.

Fast forward to current times where few carry business cards and fewer have defined titles at their jobs except for those enjoying stock options. The printing and delivery time for paper business cards is now longer than some stay at one company or in one position, so it all makes sense in our virtual world of today.

But I'll never forget when one of my colleagues used a visitor's business card as a cleaning device to get between his teeth after a lunch meeting—much to the horror of all attending except, of course, the guy involved in dental hygiene. In the end, I guess it's better that we don't exchange business cards anymore.

Lite Bites

Working on Retirement

When reflecting back on a life well lived, few people ever wished they spent more time at work. Retirement, or its little brother, resigning, is so much fun that lots of folks I know have done it more than a few times. The absolute best way to leave a job is when they provide an incentive for you to go. Rightsizing sounds so much better than downsizing, **doesn't it?**

The best incentives are accompanied by a sizable bag of money and maybe even discounts on health benefits or free training. These package deals were known as golden parachutes and were so attractive that many a worker strapped them on and jumped right out. After all, the main reason to work is for the money. After all, if you get money for *not* working, how long does it take to **agree it's a good deal?**

Resigning is the same as quitting, but sounds a lot better. **Resignment typically happens when you can't** quite draw retirement funds or Social Security yet, but you talk with your financial advisor and they convince you that your actuary tables, nest egg, anticipated spending rate, with Social Security added later on, will all intersect sometime after you die. **That's a very** good thing to hear, because it frees you to bid goodbye to a **company or boss or situation that's no longer bringing a required** level joy relative to the level of aggravation. Then you eat cake, read some nice words in some greeting cards, then on your way to the next chapter of your life.

Two weeks later, after all the chores on your list are crossed off, **you're looking for a title for that next chapter. You scrutinize your** hobbies. You ask friends and neighbors. You forget how to set the alarm. Those who are very lucky or have desirable skills seem to find opportunities dropping in their lap. My sweetie was one of those guys. Three weeks into retirement, the local university asked him to join the research team. Back to work, with guys he knew and liked, teaching topics he knew and liked, little stress, some income—what a deal! My situation was similar, but more attributed to luck of the Irish than skill.

Working a retirement job requires a fresh approach. Firstly, it must be part time, so you're not working 60 hours per week and regretting why you went back to work. You bring wisdom, so you are without fear of saying or doing the wrong thing. If you get fired, you're just back where you started. But you won't get fired, because you've seen it all by this time and understand why bosses, VPs, and the real workers do and say things that may not be in their best interest or the best interest of the company. Your coping mechanism is sharply honed to a point where you can smile and genuinely say, "OK, let's try that and see how it works," while knowing it won't.

This applies to all levels of retirement jobs, including the ones where you ask "paper or plastic" at five-minute intervals. When it gets to be less enjoyable than what's required for a retirement gig, you can just hit the *retirement* button again and have more cake.

Lite Bites

Are You Done Yet?

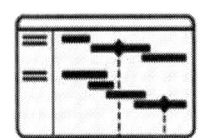

Some see engineering as a difficult career, one reserved for brainy folks who think very differently than regular people. Most engineers are technical nerds with limited social skills and dubious style choices. After spending decades working as an engineer, I can admit that I and my co-workers mostly conform to this common perception. However, I'd like to think that our technical contributions and quirky senses of humor more than compensate for blindness to social cues and inability to make small talk without reciting lines from movies.

But for all that intelligence, not one engineer I ever worked with has been able to accurately answer the question, **"When will you be done?" It doesn't matter what the task: designing something**, assembling something, writing something, testing something, or eating lunch. The elapsed-time portion of the brain cannot cohabitate with the science part in the gray matter.

As the program manager who owned the schedules, I often was the one asking this impossible question. I got back looks as if I **had two heads or spawned a third eye**. So, I'd follow up with, "Look, I'm not asking for a kidney, just tell me how long you think it will take for you to do this." Still the response would not contain a date, but rather a list of subtasks required, or all the unavailable inputs, or dates for planned vacations or doctor's appointments. Undaunted, I digress to multiple choice: "Will it take a day, a week or a month?" Still no specific answer, but something like the usual mumble of ***no way*** will it take a month would be offered. So, I settle, "OK, I'll show that it will take three weeks, and that date *should* be met with no problem, right?" "Absolutely!" is the quick answer. It appears we reached an agreement, and weekly status meetings indicate progress is right on track. But I know better, and after three weeks the Q & A dialogue of scheduling restarts for the same task.

Henry Gantt designed the Gantt Chart; a method to plan, track, and eventually miss all dates planned for a project. If you ever saw a photo of Henry Gantt, he looks really pissed. Whenever I work on Gantt charts, I feel the way he looks. Listing all the tasks to complete a complex project is a daunting task. Figuring out interdependencies of all tasks and impact of delays caused by future unknowns is impossible. Then being graded on how well you planned all this and crafting stories on why dates were missed sucks life from your soul.

During project management school, lots of time is spent on creating and updating a schedule. Come the moment that you **realize that you'll run out of time before getting the work done**, it's time to *crash* the schedule. Crash is an official term used to **squeeze an impossibly tight schedule so that you're** *really* **certain that none of the dates you plan will be met. Like when you slam on your breaks, but you still smash the car ahead of you. You can't booger with the laws of physics and make a car stop sooner than its brakes allow. Similarly, you can't stretch time. A task just won't fit between dates closer together than the time the task needs.**

Business executive, billionaire and philanthropist Sheryl Sandberg **gets credited with saying "done is better than perfect." I must have** repeated these wise words hundreds of times to engineers who felt they were eking closer to perfection in whatever design, build, or test they were working on. Every obsessive engineer will continue refinements to make something better on the quest for perfect, and that means they are never done. And that means missing the schedule. So, it's time to crash the Gantt, clean up all the resulting casualties, and move the hell on.

Foreword

As my stylist vibrated his hands wildly through my freshly cut hair, he says to me, "So, what are your plans for today?"

"I'm going to start on my book," I grinned.

He's someone who's heard it all, so I wouldn't think this would cause any reaction, and it didn't. "Really," he said flatly. "What are you writing about?"

"We'll, I just read a book written by a columnist, and my book will be patterned after that. Just short chapters. Different takes on every-day life. A collection of humorous essays on observations of the ordinary," I explained.

"You can be funny?" he squawked while his energized hands went limp and dropped to his sides. Apparently, any moron can write a book, but humor was the miracle here, especially for me.

"Well…yeah…sure," I stammered, now wondering why I didn't just tell him I was going to run some errands.

"No, really. You're funny?" he asked again with such a surprised look on his face that made me question my own talents for turning a witty phrase.

"I can be," I answered, trying desperately to think of examples. Then it came to me—I'll share that I was an actual finalist in a *Bandiera Wine Snob Essay Contest**, an honor memorialized by the winery with a certificate, a very nice T-shirt and the liberty to use the term *Award-Winning Writer* on the cover of this book. But Mike never gave me the chance to explain. He launched into how he worked with a gal who was the funniest person he ever met. To offer proof he recited her stories one after the other while remaining in his hair-stylist's zone. All the while, he continued to transform my hair from an unruly mop to a manageable do with the help of lots of manual manipulation and the application of gobs of good-smelling stuff.

And that's why I went to Mike to get my hair cut—he can carry on a conversation whether or not I'm involved. But next time when he asks what my plans are for the day, I'm saying I'm going home to clean.

*https://www.sfgate.com/food/article/Great-Bandiera-Winery-wine-snob-hunt-3155543.php

Lucky Shamrock